DK CHILDREN'S
ILLUSTRATED REFERENCE
ATLAS

Brian Delf

A Dorling Kindersley Book

LONDON, NEW YORK, MUNICH,
MELBOURNE, DELHI

Editor Lorrie Mack
Designers Adrienne Hutchinson, Andrew O'Brien
Jacket Design Neal Cobourne
DTP Designer Jill Bunyan
Design Manager Jane Thomas
Managing Editor Andrew Macintyre
Category Publisher Sue Grabham
Production Julian Deeming

The material in this book originally appeared in the
Picture Atlas of the World, published in 1996

With thanks to the original team:
Lester Cheeseman, Marcus James, Emma Johnson,
Richard Kemp, Keith Lye, Susan Peach, Roger Priddy,
Teresa Solomon, Kate Woodward, Anna Kunst,
Chris Scollen, Richard Czapnik, Struan Reid,
Cynthia Hole and Luciano Corbella

Published in Great Britain in 2002
by Dorling Kindersley Limited,
80 Strand, London WC2R 0RL
A Penguin company

This edition copyright © 2002
Dorling Kindersley, Limited
Picture Atlas of the World copyright © 1991, 1992
Dorling Kindersley, Limited

A CIP catalogue record for this book is available
from the British Library.

ISBN 0 7513 4779 5

Colour reproduction by Bright Arts, Hong Kong
Printed and bound in Hong Kong by.Toppan

Picture credits
(r = right, l = left, t = top, c = centre, b = bottom)

Australian Overseas Information Service, London 45tr, 45br;
Charles Bowman 22t, 22b, 35tr, 35br, 46t; Caribbean Tourist Office
27t; The J. Allan Cash Photolibrary 8tl, 8br, 17tl, 46br;
Lester Cheeseman 37tl, 37tr, 37bc; Chinese Tourist Office 23br;
Egyptian Tourist Office 33tr; Chris Fairclough Colour Library 15tr,
15br, 17r; French Railways Ltd 11cr; Italian State Tourist Office
20t; Norwegian Tourist Office 6tr, 7tr; Roger Priddy 8tl, 11tr, 11br,
46t; Spanish National Tourist Office 19tr; The Telegraph Colour
Library 13b; Travel Photo International 15br, 19b.

Every effort has been made to trace the copyright holders
and we apologise in advance for any unintentional omissions.
We would be pleased to insert the appropriate acknowledgment
in any subsequent edition of this book.

See our complete catalogue at
www.dk.com

CONTENTS

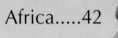
KEY TO THE MAPS

Capital city	**BERLIN** ⭐
City	● **Toronto**
Country name	**J A P A N**
Range of mountains	*A L P S*
An individual mountain with its height	Mt Everest 8,848 m
River	*Danube*
Lake	Lake Como
A building or place of special interest	Leaning Tower of Pisa
A product, animal, plant or activity that is found in the region	*Dairy cattle*

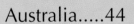

WORLD MAP

ALL THE CONTINENTS except Antarctica are divided into countries, and these vary greatly in size. The largest is the Russian Federation, which stretches across two continents – Europe and Asia. The second largest is Canada, and the third largest is China. In contrast, the smallest country is Vatican City, which lies inside the city of Rome and has an area of only .44 sq km (.17 sq miles). The Russian Federation is almost 39 million times bigger than Vatican City.

Geographers draw imaginary lines around the globe to help locate places. Lines of latitude run east/west and are measured in degrees from the Equator. Lines of longitude run north/south and are measured in degrees from the Prime Meridian.

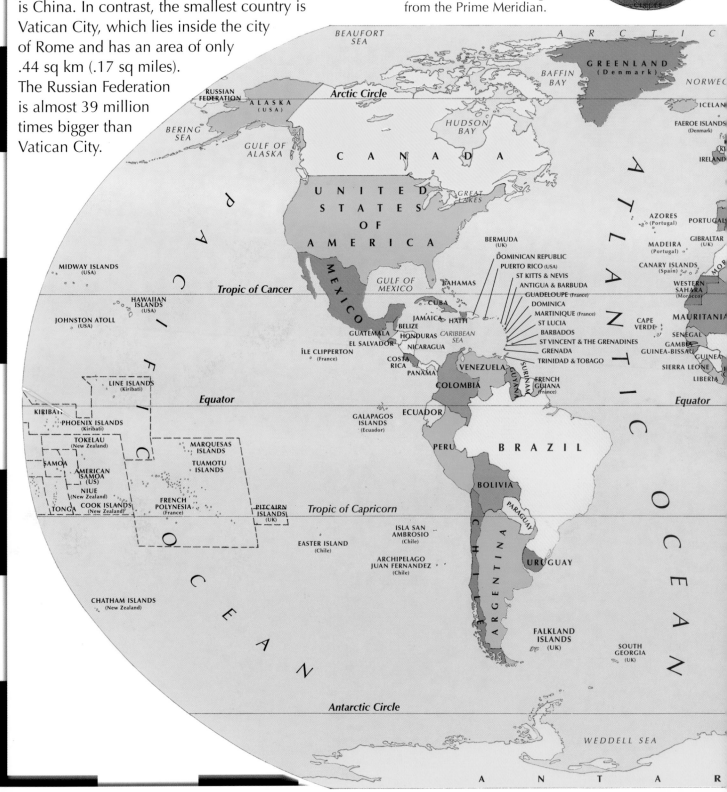

BEAUFORT SEA

GREENLAND (Denmark)

BAFFIN BAY

NORWEG

Arctic Circle

ICELAN

RUSSIAN FEDERATION

ALASKA (USA)

FAEROE ISLANDS (Denmark)

BERING SEA

HUDSON BAY

K

IRELAND

GULF OF ALASKA

C A N A D A

P

U N I T E D

GREAT LAKES

A

AZORES (Portugal)

PORTUGAL

MIDWAY ISLANDS (USA)

S T A T E S

BERMUDA (UK)

GIBRALTAR (UK)

O F

DOMINICAN REPUBLIC

MADEIRA (Portugal)

C

A M E R I C A

PUERTO RICO (USA)

CANARY ISLANDS (Spain)

Tropic of Cancer

MEXICO

GULF OF MEXICO

BAHAMAS

ST KITTS & NEVIS

ANTIGUA & BARBUDA

WESTERN SAHARA (Morocco)

HAWAIIAN ISLANDS (USA)

CUBA

GUADELOUPE (France)

MOR

DOMINICA

JOHNSTON ATOLL (USA)

JAMAICA

HAITI

MARTINIQUE (France)

MAURITANIA

BELIZE

ST LUCIA

CAPE VERDE

GUATEMALA

HONDURAS

CARIBBEAN SEA

BARBADOS

SENEGAL

ÎLE CLIPPERTON (France)

EL SALVADOR

NICARAGUA

ST VINCENT & THE GRENADINES

GAMBIA

GUINEA-BISSAU

GRENADA

GUINEA

COSTA RICA

PANAMA

TRINIDAD & TOBAGO

SIERRA LEONE

VENEZUELA

GUYANA

LIBERIA

LINE ISLANDS (Kiribati)

F

COLOMBIA

FRENCH GUIANA (France)

Equator

Equator

KIRIBATI

ECUADOR

PHOENIX ISLANDS (Kiribati)

GALAPAGOS ISLANDS (Ecuador)

C

TOKELAU (New Zealand)

MARQUESAS ISLANDS

PERU

B R A Z I L

SAMOA

TUAMOTU ISLANDS

AMERICAN SAMOA (US)

NIUE (New Zealand)

FRENCH POLYNESIA (France)

BOLIVIA

TONGA

COOK ISLANDS (New Zealand)

PITCAIRN ISLANDS (UK)

Tropic of Capricorn

PARAGUAY

O

ISLA SAN AMBROSIO (Chile)

EASTER ISLAND (Chile)

A

URUGUAY

ARCHIPELAGO JUAN FERNANDEZ (Chile)

C

CHILE

ARGENTINA

E

CHATHAM ISLANDS (New Zealand)

O

A

FALKLAND ISLANDS (UK)

SOUTH GEORGIA (UK)

C

N

E

A

Antarctic Circle

N

WEDDELL SEA

A N T A R

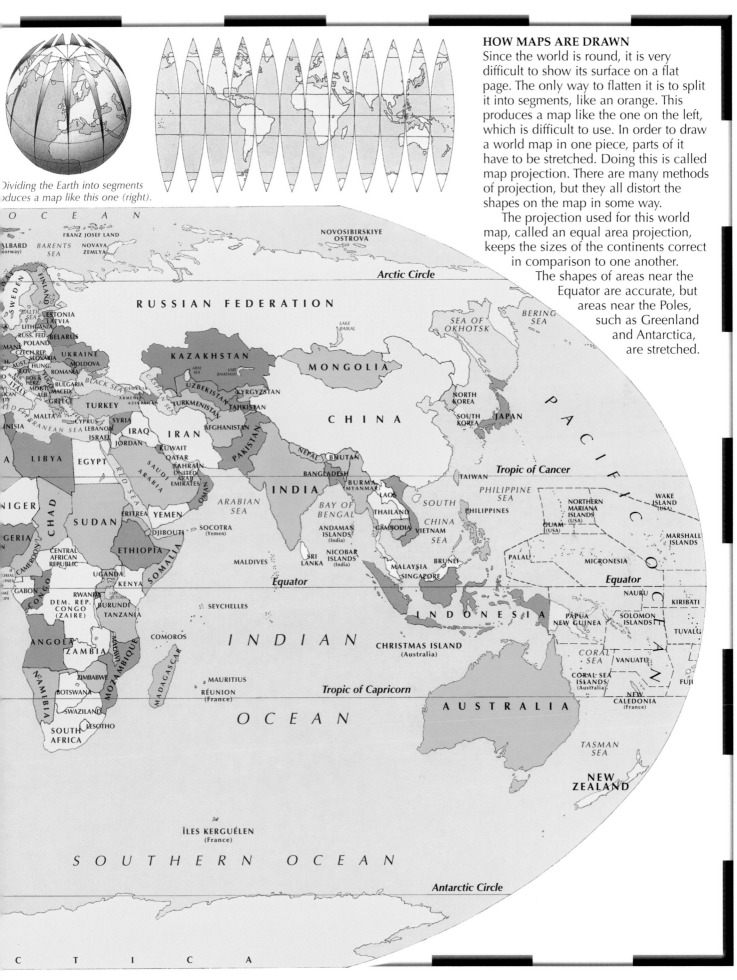

HOW MAPS ARE DRAWN

Since the world is round, it is very difficult to show its surface on a flat page. The only way to flatten it is to split it into segments, like an orange. This produces a map like the one on the left, which is difficult to use. In order to draw a world map in one piece, parts of it have to be stretched. Doing this is called map projection. There are many methods of projection, but they all distort the shapes on the map in some way.

The projection used for this world map, called an equal area projection, keeps the sizes of the continents correct in comparison to one another.

The shapes of areas near the Equator are accurate, but areas near the Poles, such as Greenland and Antarctica, are stretched.

Dividing the Earth into segments produces a map like this one (right).

O C E A N

FRANZ JOSEF LAND

NOVOSIBIRSKIYE OSTROVA

ALBARD
(Norway)
BARENTS SEA
NOVAYA ZEMLYA

Arctic Circle

SWEDEN
FINLAND

ESTONIA
LATVIA
LITHUANIA
RUSS. FED.
BELARUS

RUSSIAN FEDERATION

LAKE BAIKAL

SEA OF OKHOTSK

BERING SEA

PACIFIC OCEAN

BALTIC SEA

MANY
POLAND
CZECH REP.
SLOVAKIA
AUST.
SLOV.
HUNG.
MOLDOVA
UKRAINE

KAZAKHSTAN

ARAL SEA
LAKE BALKHASH

MONGOLIA

NORTH KOREA

ITALY
BOS &
HERZ.
MONT.
ALB.
MACED.
ROMANIA
BULGARIA
GREECE
TURKEY
BLACK SEA
GEORGIA
ARMENIA
AZERBAIJAN
CASPIAN SEA

UZBEKISTAN
TURKMENISTAN
KYRGYZSTAN
TAJIKISTAN

CHINA

SOUTH KOREA
JAPAN

MALTA
CYPRUS
SYRIA
LEBANON
ISRAEL
IRAQ
JORDAN
IRAN
AFGHANISTAN

NISIA
TERRANEAN SEA

Tropic of Cancer

LIBYA
EGYPT
KUWAIT
QATAR
BAHRAIN
UNITED ARAB EMIRATES
SAUDI ARABIA
OMAN
RED SEA

PAKISTAN
NEPAL
BHUTAN
BANGLADESH

TAIWAN

WAKE ISLAND
(USA)

NIGER
CHAD
SUDAN
ERITREA
YEMEN

INDIA
BURMA
(MYANMAR)

ARABIAN SEA
BAY OF BENGAL
LAOS
THAILAND

PHILIPPINE SEA

NORTHERN MARIANA ISLANDS
(USA)

GUAM
(USA)

MARSHALL ISLANDS

NGERIA
DJIBOUTI
SOCOTRA
(Yemen)

CENTRAL AFRICAN REPUBLIC
ETHIOPIA

ANDAMAN ISLANDS
(India)
NICOBAR ISLANDS
(India)
CAMBODIA
VIETNAM
SOUTH CHINA SEA

PHILIPPINES

PALAU

MICRONESIA

SRI LANKA

MALDIVES
MALAYSIA
SINGAPORE
BRUNEI

ORIAL
GUINEA
CIPE
GABON
UGANDA
KENYA
SOMALIA

Equator

Equator

CONGO
RWANDA
DEM. REP. CONGO
(ZAIRE)
BURUNDI
TANZANIA

SEYCHELLES

I N D O N E S I A

PAPUA NEW GUINEA

NAURU

KIRIBATI

SOLOMON ISLANDS

TUVALU

ANGOLA
ZAMBIA
COMOROS

I N D I A N

CHRISTMAS ISLAND
(Australia)

CORAL SEA
VANUATU

ZIMBABWE
MADAGASCAR
MAURITIUS
RÉUNION
(France)

CORAL SEA ISLANDS
(Australia)

FIJI

NEW CALEDONIA
(France)

NAMIBIA
BOTSWANA
SWAZILAND
MOZAMBIQUE

Tropic of Capricorn

O C E A N

AUSTRALIA

TASMAN SEA

SOUTH AFRICA
LESOTHO

ÎLES KERGUÉLEN
(France)

NEW ZEALAND

S O U T H E R N   O C E A N

Antarctic Circle

C T I C A

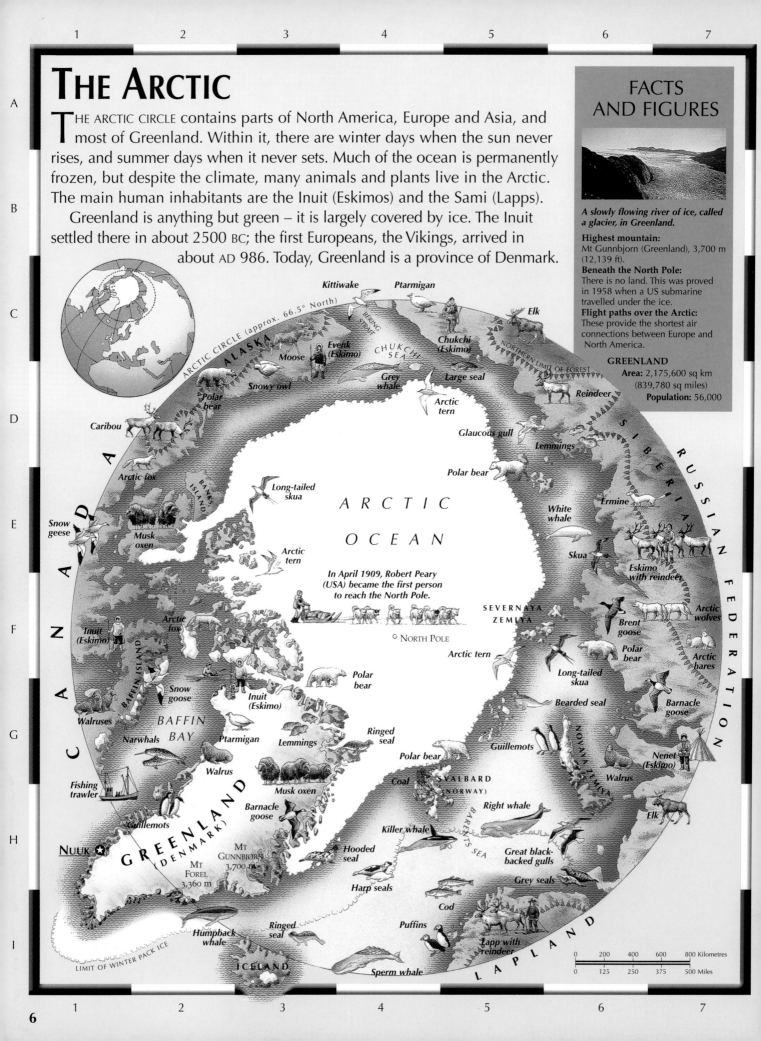

THE ARCTIC

THE ARCTIC CIRCLE contains parts of North America, Europe and Asia, and most of Greenland. Within it, there are winter days when the sun never rises, and summer days when it never sets. Much of the ocean is permanently frozen, but despite the climate, many animals and plants live in the Arctic. The main human inhabitants are the Inuit (Eskimos) and the Sami (Lapps).

Greenland is anything but green – it is largely covered by ice. The Inuit settled there in about 2500 BC; the first Europeans, the Vikings, arrived in about AD 986. Today, Greenland is a province of Denmark.

FACTS AND FIGURES

A slowly flowing river of ice, called a glacier, in Greenland.

Highest mountain:
Mt Gunnbjorn (Greenland), 3,700 m (12,139 ft).
Beneath the North Pole:
There is no land. This was proved in 1958 when a US submarine travelled under the ice.
Flight paths over the Arctic:
These provide the shortest air connections between Europe and North America.

GREENLAND
Area: 2,175,600 sq km (839,780 sq miles)
Population: 56,000

ARCTIC OCEAN

In April 1909, Robert Peary (USA) became the first person to reach the North Pole.

○ NORTH POLE

ARCTIC CIRCLE (approx. 66.5° North)

ALASKA

NORTHERN LIMIT OF FOREST

CANADA

RUSSIAN FEDERATION

SIBERIA

CHUKCHI SEA

BANKS ISLAND

BAFFIN ISLAND

BAFFIN BAY

SEVERNAYA ZEMLYA

NOVAYA ZEMLYA

BARENTS SEA

SVALBARD (NORWAY)

GREENLAND (DENMARK)

NUUK ☆

MT FOREL 3,360 m

MT GUNNBJØRN 3,700 m

ICELAND

LAPLAND

LIMIT OF WINTER PACK ICE

Labels

Kittiwake, Ptarmigan, Elk, Chukchi (Eskimo), Large seal, Evenk (Eskimo), Moose, Grey whale, Arctic tern, Snowy owl, Polar bear, Glaucous gull, Reindeer, Caribou, Lemmings, Polar bear, Arctic fox, Ermine, Long-tailed skua, White whale, Skua, Snow geese, Musk oxen, Eskimo with reindeer, Arctic tern, Arctic wolves, Brent goose, Inuit (Eskimo), Arctic fox, Polar bear, Arctic hares, Snow goose, Inuit (Eskimo), Long-tailed skua, Barnacle goose, Walruses, Bearded seal, Narwhals, Ptarmigan, Lemmings, Polar bear, Ringed seal, Guillemots, Nenet (Eskimo), Fishing trawler, Walrus, Walrus, Elk, Guillemots, Musk oxen, Barnacle goose, Coal, Right whale, Killer whale, Great black-backed gulls, Hooded seal, Grey seals, Harp seals, Cod, Puffins, Lapp with reindeer, Humpback whale, Ringed seal, Sperm whale

| 0 | 200 | 400 | 600 | 800 Kilometres |
| 0 | 125 | 250 | 375 | 500 Miles |

THE ANTARCTIC

THE ANTARCTIC HAS the world's coldest climate. Nearly all the land is covered by ice about 2,000 m (6,562 ft) thick. In summer, the ice at the edge of the sheet breaks off to form icebergs. In winter, the sea at the edge of the sheet freezes again and is called pack ice. There are very few plants, and Antarctic animals such as seals depend on the sea for their food.

No country owns Antarctica, but a number claim territory, and many have research bases there. The world's coldest temperature of -89.2°C (-128.6°F) was recorded at Vostock Station in July 1983.

FACTS AND FIGURES

The Antarctic seas are covered by drifting ice for most of the year.

Antarctica contains 90 per cent of the world's ice: If it melted, the level of the seas throughout the world would rise by 60 m (200 ft) and drown all the coastal towns and cities.

CONTINENT OF ANTARCTICA
Area: 14,000,000 sq km (5,400,000 sq miles)
Inhabitants: Only a few scientists and engineers
Climate: Bitterly cold, dry and windy

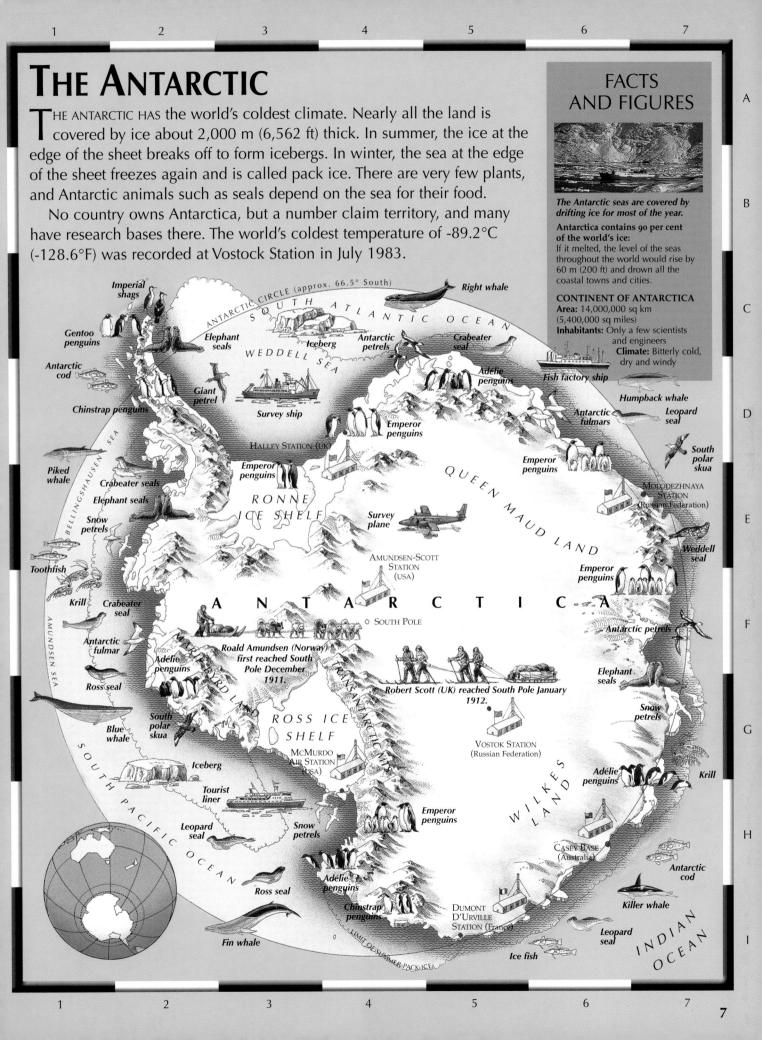

Imperial shags

Gentoo penguins

Antarctic cod

Chinstrap penguins

Piked whale

Crabeater seals

Elephant seals

Snow petrels

Toothfish

Krill

Crabeater seal

Antarctic fulmar

Adélie penguins

Ross seal

Blue whale

South polar skua

Iceberg

Tourist liner

Leopard seal

Snow petrels

Adélie penguins

Chinstrap penguins

Ross seal

Fin whale

ANTARCTIC CIRCLE (approx. 66.5° South)

SOUTH ATLANTIC OCEAN

Right whale

Elephant seals

Iceberg

Antarctic petrels

Crabeater seal

WEDDELL SEA

Adélie penguins

Fish factory ship

Giant petrel

Survey ship

Emperor penguins

HALLEY STATION (UK)

Emperor penguins

RONNE ICE SHELF

Survey plane

AMUNDSEN-SCOTT STATION (USA)

A N T A R C T I C A

○ SOUTH POLE

Roald Amundsen (Norway) first reached South Pole December 1911.

Robert Scott (UK) reached South Pole January 1912.

MARIE BYRD LAND

ROSS ICE SHELF

McMURDO AIR STATION (USA)

TRANSANTARCTIC MTS.

VOSTOK STATION (Russian Federation)

Emperor penguins

DUMONT D'URVILLE STATION (France)

Ice fish

QUEEN MAUD LAND

Emperor penguins

MOLODEZHNAYA STATION (Russian Federation)

Humpback whale

Antarctic fulmars

Leopard seal

South polar skua

Weddell seal

Emperor penguins

Antarctic petrels

Elephant seals

Snow petrels

Adélie penguins

Krill

WILKES LAND

CASEY BASE (Australia)

Antarctic cod

Killer whale

Leopard seal

INDIAN OCEAN

BELLINGSHAUSEN SEA

AMUNDSEN SEA

SOUTH PACIFIC OCEAN

LIMIT OF SUMMER PACK ICE

THE BRITISH ISLES

THE BRITISH ISLES lie off the northwest coast of Europe. They consist of two large islands – Great Britain and Ireland – surrounded by smaller ones. The British Isles are divided into two countries: the United Kingdom and Ireland. The United Kingdom (UK), also known as Britain, is made up of England, Wales, Scotland, and Northern Ireland.

During the 18th and 19th centuries, the UK was the first country to undergo an industrial revolution. It became the world's leading manufacturing and trading nation and acquired a vast empire, including Canada, Australia, New Zealand, India, and much of Africa. During the 20th century, most of these colonies became independent, although they remain linked with Britain through the Commonwealth. Today, the United Kingdom is a member of the European Union.

Until the last century, all of Ireland was part of the UK. In 1921 southern Ireland, where most people are Roman Catholic, became an independent country, while the northern part of Ireland, where the people are mainly Protestant, remained British.

FACTS AND FIGURES

The mountainous area of Snowdonia, in northern Wales, is traditionally popular for hill walking and mountaineering.

Largest cities:
London (Eng), 6,679,700;
Manchester (Eng), 2,775,000;
Birmingham (Eng), 2,551,700.
Highest mountains:
Ben Nevis (Scot), 1,343 m
(4,406 ft); Snowdon (Wales),
1,085 m (3,560 ft).
Longest rivers:
Severn (Eng–Wales), 354 km
(220 miles); Thames (Eng),
346 km (215 miles).

The parish church is the traditional centre of English country town and village life.

UNITED KINGDOM
Capital: London
Area: 244,017 sq km
(94,215 sq miles)
Population: 59,000,000
Language: English
Religion: Christian
Currency: Pound sterling
Government: Constitutional Monarchy

ENGLAND
Capital: London
Area: 130,360 sq km
(50,332 sq miles)
Population: 48,471,200

NORTHERN IRELAND
Capital: Belfast
Area: 14,121 sq km (5,452 sq miles)
Population: 1,943,400

SCOTLAND
Capital: Edinburgh
Area: 78,769 sq km (30,412 sq miles)
Population: 5,448,600

WALES
Capital: Cardiff
Area: 20,767 sq km (8,018 sq miles)
Population: 3,136,800

FACTS AND FIGURES

Much of Ireland's wealth comes from farming.

Largest metropolitan areas:
Dublin, 915,000; Cork, 174,400;
Limerick, 75,500
Highest mountain:
Carrauntoohil, 1,038 m (3,415 ft)
Longest river:
Shannon, 386 km (240 miles)

IRELAND
Capital: Dublin
Area: 70,284 sq km (27,136 sq miles)
Population: 3,700,000
Languages: English, Irish
Religion: Christian
Currency: Euro
Government: Multiparty Republic

UNITED KINGDOM

SHETLAND ISLANDS

Lerwick

Crofting (farming)

ORKNEY ISLANDS

Pilchards

Seals

Cod

Haddock

Fish packing

Oil rig

Aberdeen

Highland dress

Fishing trawler

ISLE OF LEWIS

Harris tweed

NORTH UIST

SOUTH UIST

OUTER HEBRIDES

SKYE

Sheep

Red deer

Salmon

Whisky

BEN NEVIS 1,343 m

LOCH NESS MONSTER

LOCH LOMOND

Machinery

S C O T L A N D

Glasgow

Edinburgh

BALMORAL CASTLE

EDINBURGH CASTLE

ISLE OF MULL

ISLE OF ARRAN

ISLAY

Highland cattle

GIANT'S CAUSEWAY

Golf

Sheep

Londonderry

MAP QUIZ

+ Where was the poet and playwright William Shakespeare born?

+ St George's Channel runs between which two countries?

+ What river runs through Nottingham?

+ The Vikings sailed to Ireland in wooden ships. Which Northern Irish city is famous for shipbuilding today?

+ Name the two countries divided by Hadrian's wall, built by Roman soldiers.

+ Can you find two castles in Scotland?

+ Which British island plays host to an annual motorbike race?

+ Which woollen fabric is woven on the Isle of Lewis in the Outer Hebrides?

NORTH SEA

IRISH SEA

ENGLAND

WALES

IRELAND

PENNINES

FRANCE

ENGLISH CHANNEL

BRISTOL CHANNEL

ST GEORGE'S CHANNEL

Middlesbrough

Castle Howard

Fish packing

Kingston upon Hull

HUMBER BRIDGE

Tourism

Wheat

Norwich

Fish packing

Oysters

Southend-on-Sea

Dover

CHANNEL TUNNEL

LAVENHAM GUILDHALL

Cambridge

Ipswich

ST PAUL'S CATHEDRAL

Thames

Fruit

BRIGHTON PAVILION AND PIER

Cross-channel ferry

Cricket

Leeds

Bradford

Textiles

Iron and steel

Sheffield

Coal

Trent

Nottingham

Cars

Coventry

Stratford-upon-Avon

SHAKESPEARE'S BIRTHPLACE

Oxford

Student

Machinery

LONDON

Reading

Southampton

Portsmouth

Isle of Wight

Sailing

Manchester

China

Stoke-on-Trent

Electronics

Chemicals

Birmingham

Severn

Liverpool

Football

SNOWDON 1,085 m

Sheep

BRECON BEACONS

Cardiff

Bristol

STONEHENGE

Bournemouth

SALISBURY CATHEDRAL

Tourism

Warship

Mackerel

Blackpool

Tourism

ISLE OF MAN

Douglas

Motorbike racing

Belfast

Textiles

ANGLESEY

Welsh national costume

Plaice

Swansea

Iron and steel

Puffins

Pollack

Exeter

Dairy cattle

Plymouth

China clay

ISLES OF SCILLY

GOONHILLY EARTH-STATION DISH

CHANNEL ISLANDS (UK)

Ferry

Potatoes

Lobster

Horses

IRELAND

Shannon

Limerick

Dairy cattle

CARRAUNTOOHIL 1,038 m

CASHEL MONASTERY

Cork

Petrochemicals

River cruising

Crystal

Waterford

Sailing

CUSTOMS HOUSE (DUBLIN)

Guinness

DUBLIN

IRELAND

100 Miles

150 Kilometres

0 25 50 75 100

0 50 100

9

FRANCE

FRANCE, ONE OF Europe's major farming and industrial nations, is famous for food and wine. The landscape varies dramatically from region to region and includes hot, dry areas, farmland, mountains, and forests.

France has always been powerful in Europe. In 1789 the people overthrew the king, Louis XVI, during what was later called the French Revolution. After the revolution, Napoleon, a general in the army, crowned himself Emperor. He went on to conquer most of Europe, but was defeated by the English at the Battle of Waterloo in 1815.

Today, France is a leading manufacturing country, with iron, steel, chemical, car, aeroplane, and textile industries. France is rich in farmland, and its major crops include oats, barley, wheat, flax, sugar beet, and grapes. Dairy farming is widespread and French farmers produce over 700 different types of cheese.

In terms of tourism, there are many coastal resorts, and the mountains are popular for winter sports.

MAP QUIZ

+ On which river would you find the town of Arles, with its Roman Amphitheatre?

+ The Pyrenees separate France from what other country?

+ Name the widely used condiment associated with the city of Dijon.

+ Which famous sparkling wine comes from northeastern France?

+ Can you find the site of thousands of prehistoric standing stones?

+ Which city on the edge of the Massif Central is best known for its porcelain industry?

+ On which sea are the resort towns of Nice and Cannes?

+ A winding river runs through the centre of Paris. Can you name it?

+ Pigs are used to hunt for a rare edible fungus. What is it?

+ Which city is a natural harbour at the mouth of the Seine river?

UNITED KINGDOM

ENGLISH CHANNEL

ATLANTIC OCEAN

CHA
TUN

Tourism

Ferry

Pollock

Shellfish

Fishing
Seine

Le Havre

Artichokes

Tourism

CHANNEL
ISLANDS
(UK)

MONT ST
MICHEL

BAYEUX
TAPESTRY

Crab

Calvados
(apple
brandy)

Dairy cattle

Tourism

QUIMPER
CATHEDRAL

Brest

Fishing

Le Mans

Breton
head-dress

Rennes

Quimper

STANDING
STONES
(CARNAC)

TGV high-
speed train

Tours

Warship

Loire
Lo

Nantes

CHÂTEAU DE CHENONCEAUX

Mackerel

Eels

Wine

Beef cattle

F R

FRANCE

Oysters

Tourism

Fishing

Geese

Lime

Brandy

Sailing

Gironde

CAVE PAINTING
(LASCAUX)

Pine
trees

Oysters

Bordeaux

Dordogne

Tobacco

Garonne

Wine

Pine
trees

Agen

Walnuts

Windsurfing

Boules
(French
bowls)

Oil

Brown
bear

Biarritz

Oil

Pau

Ibex
(type of goat)

PYRENEES

S P A I N

BAY OF BISCAY

| 0 | 50 | 100 | 150 | 200 Kilometres |

| 0 | 25 | 50 | 75 | 100 | 125 Miles |

A

B

C

D

E

F

G

H

I

Dunkirk

Lille

ais

BELGIUM

GERMANY

LUXEMBOURG

WORLD WAR I
MEMORIAL (VIMY)

AMIENS
CATHEDRAL

ns

Beef cattle

hion
sign

CHÂTEAU
BAS (SEDAN)

Reims

Coal

Coal

Metz

Wine

PARIS

CHÂTEAU DE
PIERREFONDS

Champagne

Potatoes

Nancy

Strasbourg

Wheat

Seine

Wild boar

Pigs

Storks

VOSGES

CHARTRES
CATHEDRAL

Orléans

Wine

SAINTE MADELEINE
(VÉZELAY)

Mustard

Dijon

CHAPEL OF NOTRE DAME
DU HAUT (RONCHAMP)

Mulhouse

SWITZERLAND

JURA

TEAU DE
MBORD

Beaune

CHÂTEAUNEUF (NIÈVRE)

Wine

Deer

N   C   E

Saône

Mâcon

orcelain

Loire

Rhône

TGV
high-speed train

MONT BLANC
4,807 M

ITALY

Hunting for
truffles

Clermont-
Ferrand

Lyon

St Etienne

Skiing

MASSIF

CENTRAL

ing

CHAPEL OF
ST MICHEL
D'AIGUILHE
(LE PUY)

Grenoble

Rhône

Mountain
climbing

ALPS

Chamois
(type of goat)

Wine

Sheep

Snails

Olives

VALENTRÉ
AHORS)

Aircraft
industry

CÉVENNES

Tourism

ouse

Montpellier

AMPHITHEATRE AT ARLES

Lavender

MONACO

Nice

Cannes

Tourism

LLED TOWN
RCASSONNE)

onne

Marseille

Fishing

Toulon

Tourism

Tourism

Flamingos

MONACO

Sailing

Warship

MEDITERRANEAN SEA

Sardines

Wine

LAR FURNACE
ODEILLO)

FACTS AND FIGURES

Amboise is one of the many historic towns along the River Loire.

Highest mountains:
Mont Blanc, 4,807 m (15,770 ft);
Les Ecrins, 4,103 m (13,461 ft);
Pic de Vignemale, 3,298 m (10,820 ft);
Mont Dore, 1,886 m (6,188 ft).

Longest rivers:
Loire, 1,005 km (625 miles);
Rhône-Saône, 812 km (505 miles);
Seine, 775 km (481 miles).

Largest cities:
Paris, 9,318,900; Lyon, 1,262,300;
Marseille, 1,231,000; Lille, 959,300;
Bordeaux, 969,400.

The high-speed TGV train, which runs between Paris and Lyon.

FRANCE
Capital: Paris
Area: 551,500 sq km
(212,936 sq miles)
Population: 59,000,000
Language: French
Religion: Christian
Currency: Euro

MONACO
Capital: Monaco
Area: 1.6 sq km (0.6 sq miles)
Population: 32,000
Language: French
Religion: Christian
Currency: Euro

Sunflowers are grown all over southern France.

CORSICA
(France)

Bastia

CORSICA

Tourism

Ajaccio

Tourism

BELGIUM, THE NETHERLANDS, AND LUXEMBOURG

BELGIUM, THE NETHERLANDS, and Luxembourg are called the "Low Countries" because they lie on the flat, low North European Plain. Almost half the Netherlands is below sea level. The saying, "God made the world, but the Dutch made the Netherlands", refers to the land they reclaimed from the sea. These areas, called polders, were drained, then protected from floods with walls, or dykes.

Belgium, the Netherlands, and Luxembourg are often called "Benelux", a short version of their names. These small countries have large populations: the Netherlands has one of the highest concentrations of people in Europe – an average of 466 in each square kilometre. All three countries are industrial, but farming, fishing and tourism are also important. Belgium and the Netherlands have been trading nations for centuries, and today, Antwerp and Rotterdam are the two busiest ports in Europe.

The Benelux countries belong to the European Union based in Brussels. Luxembourg is a centre for European organizations, while the International Courts of Justice are situated at The Hague.

BELGIUM

LUXEMBOURG

Maastricht

Mt Botrange 694 m

Iron and steel

Liège

Wild boar

CLERVAUX

Wine

LUXEMBOURG

Deer

LUXEMBOURG ★

Esch-sur-Alzette

ARDENNES FOREST

A R D E N N E S

WALZIN

Crystal

Meuse

LOUVAIN TOWN HALL

Namur

B E L G I U M

Charleroi

Sambre

Iron and steel

Pigs

Mons

EU HEADQUARTERS

Chocolates

★ BRUSSELS

Vegetables

Oudenaarde

Beef cattle

Tournai

TOURNAI CATHEDRAL

Kortrijk

F R A N C E

80 Kilometres

50 Miles

60 40
40 30
20 20
10
0 0

MAP QUIZ

✦ Which country has the same name as its capital city?

✦ What modern Dutch city is famous for the manufacture of electronic equipment and appliances?

✦ Where would you find an international centre for the cutting and selling of diamonds?

✦ The Ardennes Mountains completely cover one of the Benelux countries. Which one is it?

✦ Name the Belgian city known for both its medieval stone buildings and the exquisite lace produced there.

✦ Some of the finest chocolate in the world is exported from this region. Which country is responsible?

✦ Can you find the headquarters of the European Union?

✦ What pretty blue-and-white pottery has been manufactured in the Netherlands for hundreds of years?

FACTS AND FIGURES

The historic Belgian city of Bruges is famous for its lace.

BELGIUM
Capital: Brussels
Area: 30,514 sq km (11,781 sq miles)
Population: 10,200,000
Languages: French, Dutch, some German
Religion: Christian
Currency: Euro

LUXEMBOURG
Capital: Luxembourg
Area: 2,586 sq km (998 sq miles)
Population: 431,000
Languages: Letzeburgesch, French, German
Religion: Christian
Currencies: Euro

NETHERLANDS
Capital: Amsterdam
Seat of government: The Hague
Area: 40,844 sq km (15,770 sq miles)
Population: 15,800,000
Language: Dutch
Religion: Christian
Currency: Euro

Highest mountain:
Mt Botrange (Belg) 694 m (2,277 ft).
Lowest point:
Prins Alexander Polder (Neth), 6.7 m (22 ft) below sea level.
Largest cities:
Brussels (Belg), 950,400;
Amsterdam (Neth) 1,091,400;
Rotterdam (Neth), 1,069,400;
The Hague (Neth), 694,400

Rotterdam in the Netherlands is a major international port.

A B C D E F G H I

SCANDINAVIA

SCANDINAVIA CONSISTS OF Denmark, Norway, Sweden, and Finland in northern Europe, and the island of Iceland in the North Atlantic. Denmark is low lying farmland, whereas most of Norway is mountainous with coastal bays called fjords. Finland is full of forests and lakes, while Sweden has a varied landscape that includes forest, farmland, mountains and lakes. Central Iceland is a plateau of volcanoes, lava fields and glaciers, so most people live near the coast. Scandinavia has important natural resources, including timber, fish, iron ore and oil and natural gas in the North Sea. Today, the Scandinavian countries are all industrial, and their people enjoy a high standard of living.

MAP QUIZ

✦ Lego building blocks were invented in which Scandinavian country, where there is a theme park dedicated to them?

✦ Where would you see the statue of the Little Mermaid?

✦ Can you identify two Scandinavian countries that have large paper-making industries?

✦ Name a region where you can find reindeer like the ones associated with the legend of Father Christmas.

✦ In which country are Volvo cars manufactured?

✦ A large mountain range runs along the border between Norway and Sweden. What is it called?

ATLANTIC OCEAN

NORWEGIAN SEA

NORWAY

Fishing trawler

Salmon

Coastal express

Trondheim

Skiing

STAVE CHURCH (BORGUND)

Wolverine

NOR

GALDHØPIGGEN 2,469 m

Mountain climbing

Bergen

CITY HALL (OSLO)

Ski jumping

Electric power

Stavanger

Folk costume

OSLO

Paper

Karlstad

LAKE VÄNERN

VÄ

Oil and gas

Sheep

SKAGERRAK

STATUE OF POSEIDON

Herrings

Borås

Herrings

Gothenburg

Volvo car

KATTEGAT

Dairy cattle

KRONBORG C. (HELSINGO

LEGOLAND

DENMARK

Aarhus

COPENHAGEN

NORTH SEA

Esbjerg

Malmö

Pigs

LITTLE MERMAID STATUE (COPENHAGEN)

GERMANY

ICELAND

Puffins

Sheep

GODAFOSS WATERFALL

VATNAJÖKULL (ICE SHEET)

Herrings

STROKKUR GEYSER

REYKJAVIK

Cod

ICELAND

DENMARK

NORTH CAPE

BARENTS SEA

Fishing trawler

Reindeer

Tromso

Cod

VESTERÅLEN

LOFOTEN ISLANDS

Narvik

Sami (Lapps)

LAPLAND

Wolves

Puffins

KJÖLEN MTS

Iron ore

Salmon

Elk

Birch tree

FINLAND

Lynx

SWEDEN

Cross-country skiing

Sailing

Oulu

Sauna

Umeå

Norway spruce

Salmon

GULF OF BOTHNIA

Furs

FINLAND

Scots pine

Folk costume

TAMPERE CATHEDRAL

Paper

Herrings

Trout

Model horse (Dalarna)

Tampere

HELSINKI RAILWAY STATION

DROTTNINGHOLM PALACE

Lahti

Turku

Potatoes

Uppsala

ALAND ISLANDS

HELSINKI

STOCKHOLM

Ice-breaker ship

GULF OF FINLAND

CITY HALL (STOCKHOLM)

ESTONIA

RUSSIAN FEDERATION

Rune stone (ancient inscription)

BALTIC SEA

GOTLAND

ÖLAND

Guillemots

LATVIA

SWEDEN

0 50 100 150 200 250 Kilometres
0 50 100 150 Miles

FACTS AND FIGURES

Scandinavia's forests support large timber and paper industries.

Highest mountain:
Galdhøpiggen (Norway), 2,469 m (8,100 ft).

Largest lake:
Lake Vänern (Sweden), 5,580 sq km (2,155 sq miles).

Largest cities:
Copenhagen (Denmark), 1,342,700; Stockholm (Sweden), 1,450,000; Helsinki (Finland), 1,040,000; Oslo (Norway) 720,000; Gothenborg (Sweden) 710,900

Copenhagen has been a port and trading centre since the Middle Ages.

DENMARK
Capital: Copenhagen
Area: 43,077 sq km (16,632 sq miles)
Population: 5,300,000
Language: Danish
Religion: Christian
Currency: Danish krone
Government: Constitutional Monarchy

FINLAND
Capital: Helsinki
Area: 338,127 sq km (130,551 sq miles)
Population: 5,200,000
Languages: Finnish, Swedish, Lappish
Religion: Christian
Currency: Euro
Government: Multiparty Republic

ICELAND
Capital: Reykjavik
Area: 103,000 sq km (39,768 sq miles)
Population: 281,000
Language: Icelandic
Religion: Christian
Currency: Icelandic krona
Government: Constitutional Republic

NORWAY
Capital: Oslo
Area: 323,895 sq km (125,056 sq miles)
Population: 4,500,000
Languages: Norwegian, Lappish
Religion: Christian
Currency: Norwegian krona
Government: Constitutional Monarchy

SWEDEN
Capital: Stockholm
Area: 440,945 sq km (170,250 sq miles)
Population: 8,900,000
Languages: Swedish, Lappish
Religion: Christian
Currency: Swedish krone
Government: Constitutional Monarchy

FINLAND

GERMANY, AUSTRIA, AND SWITZERLAND

THE LANDSCAPE IN this region is crossed by two of Europe's longest rivers: the Rhine, flowing north to the North Sea, and the Danube, flowing east to the Black Sea.

For hundreds of years, the area now called Germany consisted of small independent states, which were first united in 1871. Germany rapidly became an important power, but after World War II, the country was split into two parts: the Federal Republic of Germany (West Germany) and the communist German Democratic Republic (East Germany). This split lasted for over 40 years. The two German states were reunited in 1990, following the collapse of communism in East Germany. Today, Germany is the wealthiest country in Europe and one of the world's foremost industrial nations.

To the south lie the mountainous countries of Austria and Switzerland, which both rely heavily on tourism. Switzerland is famous for watches and scientific instruments, and it is also a major business centre. Becoming neutral in 1815, it has stayed out of every war affecting Europe since then. Austria is also neutral. The tiny country of Liechtenstein is only about 24 km (15 miles) long and 8 km (5 miles) wide.

| 0 | 50 | 100 | 150 | 200 Kilometres |
| 0 | 25 | 50 | 75 | 100 | 125 Miles |

The Alps

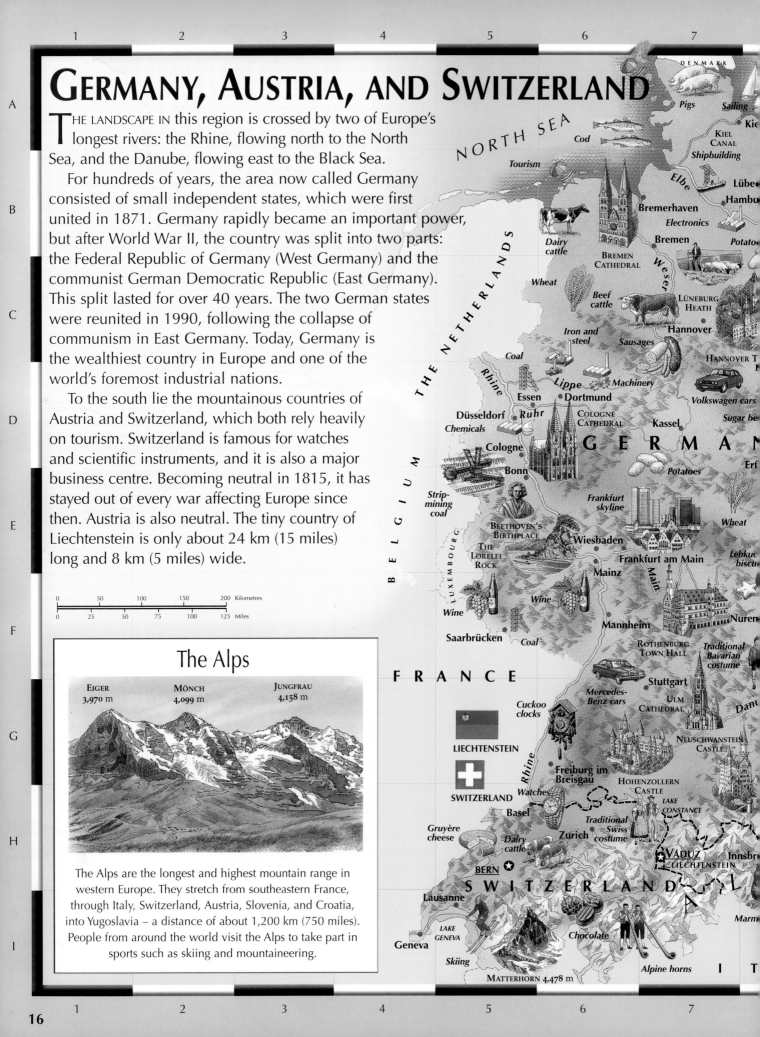

| EIGER 3,970 m | MÖNCH 4,099 m | JUNGFRAU 4,158 m |

The Alps are the longest and highest mountain range in western Europe. They stretch from southeastern France, through Italy, Switzerland, Austria, Slovenia, and Croatia, into Yugoslavia – a distance of about 1,200 km (750 miles). People from around the world visit the Alps to take part in sports such as skiing and mountaineering.

DENMARK

NORTH SEA

Pigs

Sailing

Kie

Cod

KIEL CANAL

Shipbuilding

Tourism

Elbe

Lübe

Hambu

Electronics

Bremerhaven

Bremen

Potato

Dairy cattle

Weser

BREMEN CATHEDRAL

THE NETHERLANDS

Wheat

Beef cattle

LÜNEBURG HEATH

Hannover

HANNOVER T

Iron and steel

Sausages

Coal

Rhine

Lippe

Machinery

Essen

Dortmund

Volkswagen cars

Düsseldorf

Ruhr

COLOGNE CATHEDRAL

Kassel

Sugar be

BELGIUM

Chemicals

G E R M A N

Cologne

Potatoes

Erf

Bonn

LUXEMBOURG

Strip-mining coal

Frankfurt skyline

BEETHOVEN'S BIRTHPLACE

Wheat

THE LORELEI ROCK

Wiesbaden

Lebkuc biscu

Mainz

Frankfurt am Main

Main

Wine

Wine

Saarbrücken

Mannheim

Nuren

Coal

ROTHENBURG TOWN HALL

Traditional Bavarian costume

FRANCE

Mercedes-Benz cars

Stuttgart

Cuckoo clocks

ULM CATHEDRAL

Dan

LIECHTENSTEIN

NEUSCHWANSTEIN CASTLE

SWITZERLAND

Rhine

Freiburg im Breisgau

HOHENZOLLERN CASTLE

Watches

LAKE CONSTANCE

Basel

Traditional Swiss costume

VADUZ LIECHTENSTEIN

Innsbr

Gruyère cheese

Zurich

Dairy cattle

BERN

S W I T Z E R L A N D

Lausanne

Marm

Chocolate

LAKE GENEVA

Geneva

Alpine horns

I T

Skiing

MATTERHORN 4,478 m

BALTIC SEA

RÜGEN

...hipbuilding

Rostock
Storks

Sheep

...verin

Dairy cattle

BRANDENBURG GATE

Sugar beet

Machinery

★ BERLIN

Potsdam

Magdeburg

Pigs

Elbe

Poultry

Halle

Leipzig

...ping
...ing
...al

Chemnitz

Zwickau

Iron and steel

Textiles
Dresden

ZWINGER PALACE

GERMANY (flag)

POLAND

FACTS AND FIGURES

Vienna's Belvedere Castle was built for the Habsburg family.

Longest rivers:
Danube, 2,858 km (1,776 miles); Rhine, 1,320 km (820 miles).

Largest lakes:
Lake Geneva (Switz-Fr), 580 sq km (224 sq miles); Lake Constance (Ger-Switz-Aust), 539 sq km (208 sq miles).

Largest cities:
Berlin (Ger), 3,446,000; Hamburg (Ger), 1,660,700; Vienna (Aust), 1,539,900; Munich (Ger), 1,236,500; Zurich (Switz), 1,158,100; Cologne (Ger), 955,500; Frankfurt (Ger), 647,200; Essen (Ger), 626,100.

World's tallest spire:
The cathedral of Ulm in Germany has the world's tallest church spire. It is 161 m (528 ft) high.

Busiest canal:
Germany's Kiel Canal is the busiest in the world. Every year, about 45,000 ships use it to pass between the North Sea and the Baltic Sea.

World's longest road tunnel:
St Gotthard tunnel in Switzerland runs under the Alps, and is 16.32 km (10.14 miles) long.

World's biggest roof:
The glass roof over the Olympic Stadium in Munich measures 85,000 sq m (914,940 sq ft).

Cows grazing in the Alps give milk for Swiss chocolate.

AUSTRIA
Capital: Vienna
Area: 83,853 sq km (32,375 sq miles)
Population: 8,200,000
Language: German
Religion: Christian
Currency: Euro
Government: Multiparty Republic

GERMANY
Capital: Berlin
Area: 356,910 sq km (137,804 sq miles)
Population: 82,200,000
Language: German
Religion: Christian
Currency: Euro
Government: Multiparty Republic

LIECHTENSTEIN
Capital: Vaduz
Area: 160 sq km (62 sq miles)
Population: 32,000
Language: German
Religion: Christian
Currency: Swiss franc
Government: Constititional Monarchy

SWITZERLAND
Capital: Bern
Area: 41,293 sq km (15,943 sq miles)
Population: 7,400,000
Languages: German, French, Italian
Religion: Christian
Currency: Swiss franc
Government: Federal Republic

CZECH REPUBLIC

REGENSBURG CATHEDRAL

Regensburg

Cakes

Beer

Sugar beet

Electronics

Linz

Lipizzaner horses

VIENNA OPERA HOUSE

Danube

...unich

Dairy cattle

★ VIENNA

Iron and steel

SLOVAKIA

HOHENSALZBURG CASTLE

Salzburg

MOZART'S BIRTHPLACE

Violins

Great white heron

MARIA-HILF-KIRCHE (GRAZ)

A U S T R I A

Edelweiss

Graz

Skiing

HUNGARY

AUSTRIA (flag)

Chamois (type of goat)

Mountain climbing

...A L Y

S L O V E N I A

MAP QUIZ

✦ What mountain range extends across Germany, Austria and Switzerland?

✦ By which river would you find the Lorelei Rock, where a legendary water nymph lured sailors to their death?

✦ The birthplace of Wolfgang Amadeus Mozart is now the home of an important music festival. Which city is it?

✦ Name two important car manufacturers that are based in Germany.

✦ Which city is famous for its Opera House, its rich cakes and its elegant Lipizzaner horses?

✦ In which country would you be able to hear the distinctive sound of alpine horns?

✦ List four German cities that have beautiful old cathedrals shown on the map.

✦ Identify the country most closely associated with the white edelweiss flower.

✦ Where is the huge Matterhorn mountain?

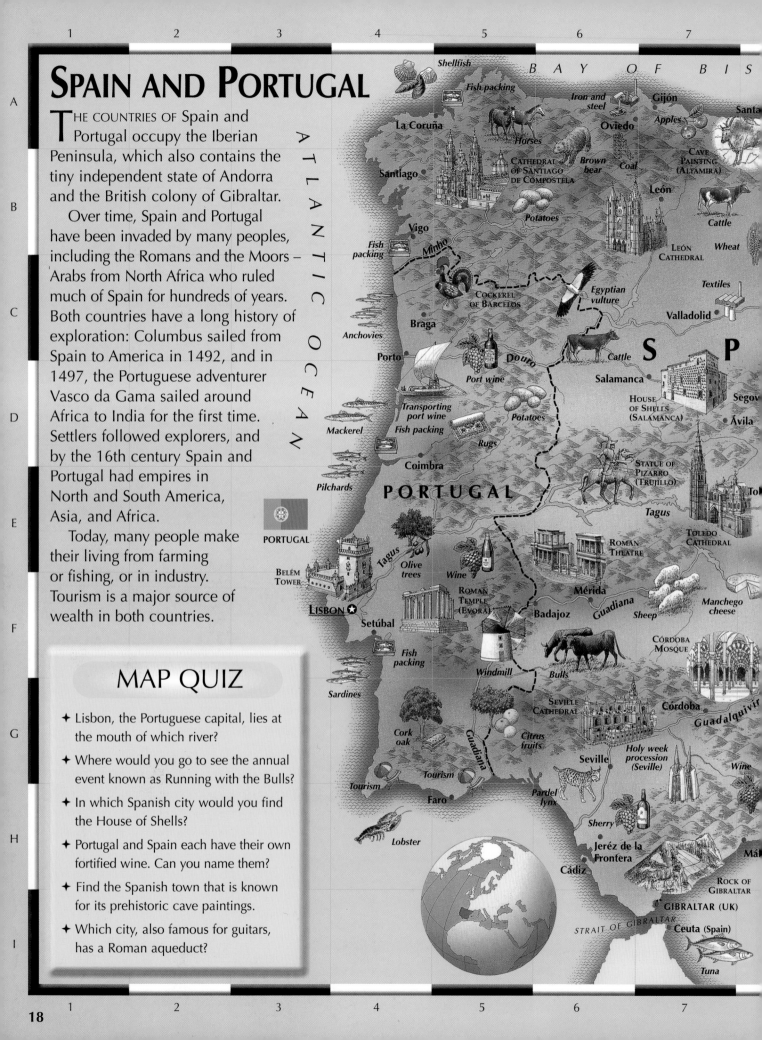

SPAIN AND PORTUGAL

THE COUNTRIES OF Spain and Portugal occupy the Iberian Peninsula, which also contains the tiny independent state of Andorra and the British colony of Gibraltar.

Over time, Spain and Portugal have been invaded by many peoples, including the Romans and the Moors – Arabs from North Africa who ruled much of Spain for hundreds of years. Both countries have a long history of exploration: Columbus sailed from Spain to America in 1492, and in 1497, the Portuguese adventurer Vasco da Gama sailed around Africa to India for the first time. Settlers followed explorers, and by the 16th century Spain and Portugal had empires in North and South America, Asia, and Africa.

Today, many people make their living from farming or fishing, or in industry. Tourism is a major source of wealth in both countries.

PORTUGAL

MAP QUIZ

✦ Lisbon, the Portuguese capital, lies at the mouth of which river?

✦ Where would you go to see the annual event known as Running with the Bulls?

✦ In which Spanish city would you find the House of Shells?

✦ Portugal and Spain each have their own fortified wine. Can you name them?

✦ Find the Spanish town that is known for its prehistoric cave paintings.

✦ Which city, also famous for guitars, has a Roman aqueduct?

ATLANTIC OCEAN

BAY OF BIS

Shellfish
Fish packing
Iron and steel
Gijón
Santa
La Coruña
Apples
Horses
Oviedo
CAVE PAINTING (ALTAMIRA)
CATHEDRAL OF SANTIAGO DE COMPOSTELA
Brown bear
Coal
Santiago
León
Vigo
Potatoes
Cattle
Fish packing
Minho
LEÓN CATHEDRAL
Wheat
Egyptian vulture
Textiles
COCKEREL OF BARCELOS
Braga
Anchovies
Cattle
Valladolid
S P
Porto
Douro
Salamanca
Port wine
Segov
HOUSE OF SHELLS (SALAMANCA)
Transporting port wine
Potatoes
Ávila
Mackerel
Fish packing
Rugs
STATUE OF PIZARRO (TRUJILLO)
Coimbra
To
Pilchards
Tagus
PORTUGAL
TOLEDO CATHEDRAL
Tagus
ROMAN THEATRE
Olive trees
Wine
BELÉM TOWER
ROMAN TEMPLE (ÉVORA)
Mérida
Manchego cheese
LISBON
Badajoz
Guadiana
Sheep
Setúbal
CÓRDOBA MOSQUE
Fish packing
Windmill
Bulls
SEVILLE CATHEDRAL
Córdoba
Sardines
Guadalquivir
Citrus fruits
Cork oak
Tourism
Seville
Holy week procession (Seville)
Wine
Tourism
Guadiana
Faro
Pardel lynx
Sherry
Lobster
Jeréz de la Frontera
Má
Cádiz
ROCK OF GIBRALTAR
GIBRALTAR (UK)
STRAIT OF GIBRALTAR
Ceuta (Spain)
Tuna

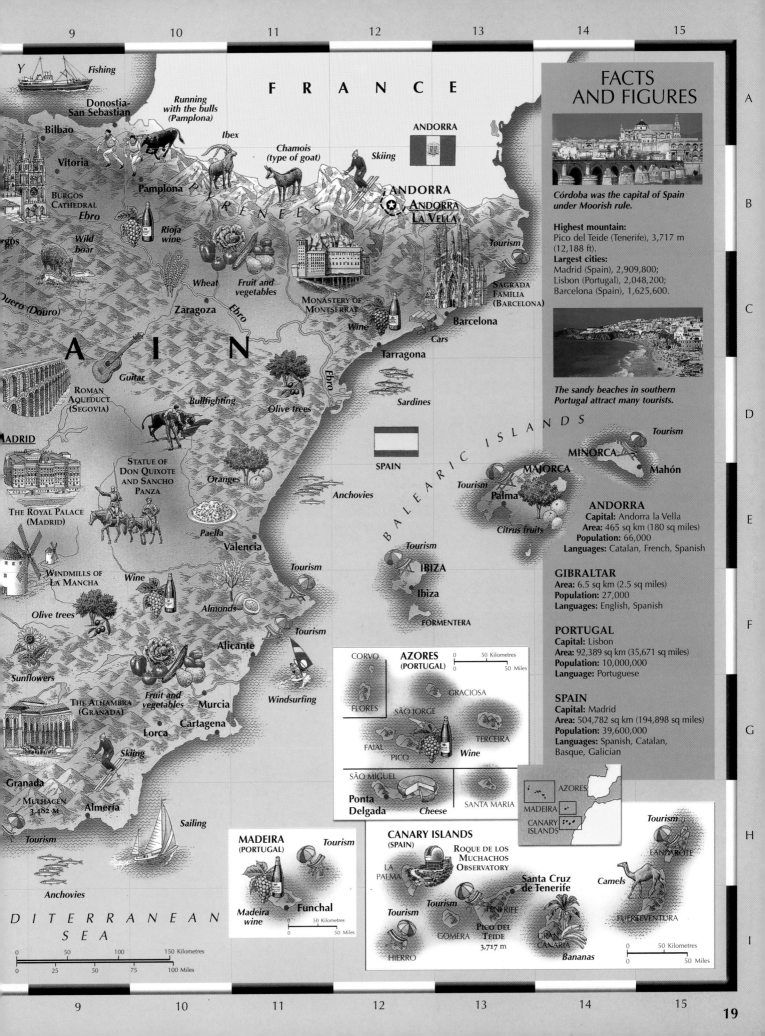

FRANCE

Fishing
Donostia-San Sebastián
Bilbao
Vitoria
BURGOS CATHEDRAL
Ebro
Wild boar
Burgos
Duero (Douro)
Running with the bulls (Pamplona)
Pamplona
Rioja wine
Wheat
Fruit and vegetables
P Y R E N E E S
Ibex
Chamois (type of goat)
Skiing
ANDORRA
ANDORRA
ANDORRA LA VELLA

Tourism

A I N
ROMAN AQUEDUCT (SEGOVIA)
Guitar
Zaragoza
Ebro
MONASTERY OF MONTSERRAT
Wine
Ebro
SAGRADA FAMILIA (BARCELONA)
Barcelona
Cars
Tarragona

MADRID
THE ROYAL PALACE (MADRID)
Bullfighting
Olive trees
Sardines
STATUE OF DON QUIXOTE AND SANCHO PANZA
Oranges
Anchovies
SPAIN
B A L E A R I C   I S L A N D S
Tourism
MINORCA
Mahón
MAJORCA
Palma
Tourism
Citrus fruits

WINDMILLS OF LA MANCHA
Wine
Paella
Valencia
Tourism
Tourism
IBIZA
Ibiza
FORMENTERA

Olive trees
Sunflowers
Almonds
THE ALHAMBRA (GRANADA)
Fruit and vegetables
Murcia
Alicante
Tourism
Windsurfing
Cartagena
Lorca
Skiing
Granada
MULHACÉN 3,482 M
Almería
Sailing
Tourism
Anchovies

M E D I T E R R A N E A N   S E A

FACTS AND FIGURES

Córdoba was the capital of Spain under Moorish rule.

Highest mountain:
Pico del Teide (Tenerife), 3,717 m (12,188 ft).
Largest cities:
Madrid (Spain), 2,909,800;
Lisbon (Portugal), 2,048,200;
Barcelona (Spain), 1,625,600.

The sandy beaches in southern Portugal attract many tourists.

ANDORRA
Capital: Andorra la Vella
Area: 465 sq km (180 sq miles)
Population: 66,000
Languages: Catalan, French, Spanish

GIBRALTAR
Area: 6.5 sq km (2.5 sq miles)
Population: 27,000
Languages: English, Spanish

PORTUGAL
Capital: Lisbon
Area: 92,389 sq km (35,671 sq miles)
Population: 10,000,000
Language: Portuguese

SPAIN
Capital: Madrid
Area: 504,782 sq km (194,898 sq miles)
Population: 39,600,000
Languages: Spanish, Catalan, Basque, Galician

AZORES (PORTUGAL)
0 — 50 Kilometres
0 — 50 Miles
CORVO
FLORES
GRACIOSA
SÃO JORGE
FAIAL
PICO
Wine
TERCEIRA
SÃO MIGUEL
Ponta Delgada
Cheese
SANTA MARIA

AZORES
MADEIRA
CANARY ISLANDS

MADEIRA (PORTUGAL)
Tourism
Madeira wine
Funchal
0 — 50 Kilometres
0 — 50 Miles

CANARY ISLANDS (SPAIN)
LA PALMA
ROQUE DE LOS MUCHACHOS OBSERVATORY
Santa Cruz de Tenerife
Tourism
Tourism
TENERIFE
GOMERA
Pico del Teide 3,717 m
HIERRO
GRAN CANARIA
Bananas
Tourism
LANZAROTE
Camels
FUERTEVENTURA
0 — 50 Kilometres
0 — 50 Miles

0 — 50 — 100 — 150 Kilometres
0 — 25 — 50 — 75 — 100 Miles

ITALY

THE EASILY RECOGNIZABLE boot shape of Italy is a 800-km (500-mile) long peninsula that stretches south into the Mediterranean Sea. Most of the country is mountainous or hilly, and in the north, the Alps form a barrier between Italy and the rest of Europe. Running down the spine of the country are the Apennines, rugged mountains dotted with villages and towns that haven't changed for centuries. The Mediterranean islands of Sicily and Sardinia are also part of Italy.

Modern Italy, with Rome as its capital, only came into existence in 1870. Before then, the area was a patchwork of independent city states, and these states can still be seen today in Italy's 20 "regions". Two have remained independent – the Vatican City in Rome and the Republic of San Marino in northeastern Italy.

In Roman times, the Italian peninsula was the centre of a great empire, and the remains of Roman roads and buildings can still be seen. In the 14th–16th centuries, Italy was the centre of an important artistic movement called the Renaissance. Many beautiful paintings, sculptures, buildings, and poems were produced here, and among Italy's most famous Renaissance artists and writers were Michelangelo, Leonardo da Vinci, Raphael, and Dante. Today, millions of tourists each year visit Italy's ancient cities and art treasures.

Modern Italy has large steel, chemical, textile, and car industries, and farming is still important: wheat, corn, rice, grapes and olives are the main crops. Fishing plays a part too, with fresh seafood coming into many small coastal ports.

FACTS AND FIGURES

ITALY
Capital: Rome
Area: 301,268 sq km
(116,320 sq miles)
Population: 57,300,000
Language: Italian
Religion: Christian
Currency: Euro
Government: Multiparty Republic

MALTA
Capital: Valletta
Area: 316 sq km (122 sq miles)
Population: 389,000
Languages: Maltese, English
Religion: Christian
Currency: Maltese Lira
Government: Multiparty Republic

SAN MARINO
Capital: San Marino
Area: 61 sq km (23 sq miles)
Population: 26,000
Language: Italian
Religion: Christian
Currency: Euro
Government: Multiparty Republic

VATICAN CITY
Area: 0.44 sq km (0.17 sq miles)
Population: 1,000

A horse race called the Palio takes place in Siena each year.

Venice is built on islands and has many canals in place of streets.

Highest mountains:
Mont Blanc (It-Fr), 4,807 m
(15,770 ft); Monte Rosa
(It-Switz), 4,634 m (15,203 ft).
Longest river:
Po, 672 km (418 miles).
Largest lakes:
Lake Garda, 370 sq km
(143 sq miles); Lake Maggiore,
212 sq km (82 sq miles); Lake
Como, 145 sq km (55 sq miles).
Largest cities:
Milan, 3,750,000; Rome,
3,175,000; Naples, 2,875,000;
Turin, 1,550,000.

SWITZERLAND

AUSTRIA

FRANCE

SLOVENIA

CROATIA

ALPS

APENNINES

LIGURIAN SEA

MONTE ROSA
4,634 m

MONT BLANC
4,807 m

PINNACLES OF THE
DOLOMITES

Chamois
(type of goat)

Ibex
(type of goat)

Marmots

Skiing

Udine

Trieste

Bolzano

Trento

Verona

Mantua

Bergamo

Brescia

Violins

Cremona

Parmesan
cheese

Parma

Modena

Bologna

Ravenna

Ferrara

Padua

Venice

ST MARK'S
SQUARE

Venetian
gondolier

Wine

Ferrari
cars

Po

Adige

Po

Monza

Milan

Como

LAKE
COMO

LAKE
MAGGIORE

LAKE
GARDA

MILAN
CATHEDRAL

Rice

Turin

Fiat cars

Wine

Olive
trees

Genoa

La Spezia

Livorno

Pisa

LEANING TOWER

Arno

Florence

FLORENCE
CATHEDRAL

Rimini

OLD TOWN OF
SAN MARINO

SAN
MARINO

Ancona

SANTA

Sole

Cruise
liner

Tourism

Tourism

Tourism

Tourism

Tourism

Shellfish

Marble
quarry

Sardines

Ferry boat

Venice is built on islands and has many canals in place of streets.

MAP QUIZ

✦ Where would you find the live volcano of Mount Etna?

✦ Name the five seas that surround Italy.

✦ Which river runs through Florence?

✦ In what city are Fiat cars manufactured?

✦ Which Italian island gave its name to a small fish that lives in the surrounding waters?

✦ Gladiators once fought to the death in the Colosseum. Where is it?

✦ Which city in the Alps shares its name with the lake it lies on?

ITALY

SAN MARINO

VATICAN CITY

MALTA

ADRIATIC SEA

TYRRHENIAN SEA

IONIAN SEA

MEDITERRANEAN SEA

ITALY

CORSICA

SARDINIA

SICILY

MALTA

GOZO

PANTELLERIA

USTICA

ELBA

GIGLIO

APENNINES

ROME

VATICAN CITY

Naples

Salerno

Foggia

Bari

Brindisi

Taranto

Crotone

Reggio di Calabria

Messina

Palermo

Syracuse

Ragusa

Agrigento

Catania

Pescara

VALLETTA

CAGLIARI

Tiber

VESUVIUS 1,277 m

MT. ETNA 3,323 m

STROMBOLI

Aeolian Islands

CASTEL DEL MONTE

THE COLOSSEUM (ROME)

Temple of PAESTUM

TEMPLE OF CASTOR AND POLLOX

BRONZES OF RIACE

ISCHIA

CAPRI

Garlic

Pasta

Wine

Olives

Octopus

Sea bream

Red mullet

Tobacco

Almonds

Pizza

Shellfish

Steel

Crabs

Wine

Oysters

Citrus fruits

Olive trees

Goats

Garfish

Anchovies

Swordfish

Tourism

Citrus fruits

Wine

Carob tree

Prawns

Ferry boat

Tuna

Sardines

Grey mullet

Scuba diving

Tourism

Crayfish

Petro-chemicals

Olive trees

Goats and Sheep

Citrus fruits

Wine

Tourism

150 Kilometres

100 Miles

21

CENTRAL AND EASTERN EUROPE

THIS REGION HAS ALWAYS been subject to change, and the borders have shifted many times. After World War II, all the countries apart from Greece became part of the "Eastern Bloc". They had communist regimes and ties with the former USSR. In recent years, however, many nations have established democratic governments with links to Western Europe.

The north of the region is dominated by Poland, which is rich in coal and copper, with large iron, steel, shipbuilding and textile industries. Farming is also important: the main crops are potatoes, wheat, and sugar beet.

To the south lie the Czech Republic and Slovakia, which until 1993 were one country – Czechoslovakia – with two peoples (Czechs and Slovaks) speaking different languages.

Below this is southeastern Europe: Greece, Albania, Bosnia and Herzegovina, Croatia, Slovenia, Macedonia, Yugoslavia, Bulgaria, Romania, and Hungary. Many of these countries were only formed at the end of the two World Wars. More recently, the republics of Bosnia and Herzegovina, Croatia, Macedonia and Slovenia broke away from Yugoslavia and were recognized as independent countries.

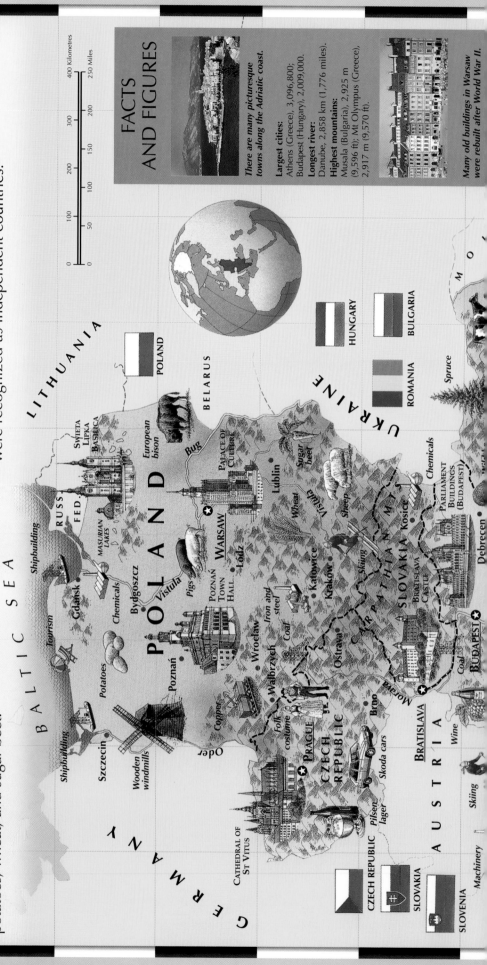

FACTS AND FIGURES

There are many picturesque towns along the Adriatic coast.

Largest cities:
Athens (Greece), 3,096,800;
Budapest (Hungary), 2,009,000.
Longest river:
Danube, 2,858 km (1,776 miles).
Highest mountains:
Musala (Bulgaria), 2,925 m
(9,596 ft); Mt Olympus (Greece),
2,917 m (9,570 ft).

Many old buildings in Warsaw were rebuilt after World War II.

400 Kilometres
250 Miles

0   50   100   150   200   300

0   100   200   400

POLAND

HUNGARY

ROMANIA

BULGARIA

CZECH REPUBLIC

SLOVAKIA

SLOVENIA

Machinery

Skiing

GERMANY

CATHEDRAL OF ST VITUS

Pilsen lager

Folk costume

PRAGUE

CZECH REPUBLIC

Brno

Skoda cars

Wine

AUSTRIA

Morava

BRATISLAVA

BUDAPEST

Copper

Wałbrzych

Coal

Ostrava

Košice

SLOVAKIA

BRATISLAVA CASTLE

PARLIAMENT BUILDINGS (BUDAPEST)

Debrecen

Chemicals

C A R P A T H I A N   M T S

Kraków

Katowice

Iron and steel

Skiing

Sheep

Sugar beet

Wrocław

Coal

Wieliczka

Wheat

Oder

Wooden windmills

Shipbuilding

Szczecin

BALTIC SEA

Tourism

Potatoes

Gdańsk

Shipbuilding

Poznań

POZNAŃ TOWN HALL

Pigs

Vistula

Bydgoszcz

Chemicals

P O L A N D

WARSAW

Łódź

Lublin

PALACE OF CULTURE

Bug

European bison

ŚWIĘTA LIPKA BASILICA

MASURIAN LAKES

RUSS. FED.

LITHUANIA

BELARUS

UKRAINE

Spruce

M O

Vistula

Country Information

ALBANIA
Capital: Tirana
Area: 28,748 sq km (11,099 sq miles)
Population: 3,300,000

BOSNIA & HERZEGOVINA
Capital: Sarajevo
Area: 51,129 sq km (19,741 sq miles)
Population: 4,000,000

BULGARIA
Capital: Sofia
Area: 110,912 sq km (42,823 sq miles)
Population: 8,200,000

CROATIA
Capital: Zagreb
Area: 56,538 sq km (21,829 sq miles)
Population: 4,500,000

CZECH REPUBLIC
Capital: Prague
Area: 78,864 sq km (30,449 sq miles)
Population: 10,200,000

GREECE
Capital: Athens
Area: 131,990 sq km (50,961 sq miles)
Population: 10,600,000

HUNGARY
Capital: Budapest
Area: 93,032 sq km (35,919 sq miles)
Population: 10,000,000

MACEDONIA
Capital: Skopje
Area: 25,713 sq km (9,928 sq miles)
Population: 2,000,000

POLAND
Capital: Warsaw
Area: 312,685 sq km (120,728 sq miles)
Population: 38,800,000

ROMANIA
Capital: Bucharest
Area: 237,500 sq km (91,699 sq miles)
Population: 22,300,000

SLOVAKIA
Capital: Bratislava
Area: 49,035 sq km (18,932 sq miles)
Population: 5,400,000

SLOVENIA
Capital: Ljubljana
Area: 20,251 sq km (7,819 sq miles)
Population: 2,000,000

YUGOSLAVIA
Capital: Belgrade
Area: 102,173 sq km (39,449 sq miles)
Population: 10,600,00

MAP QUIZ

- The goddess Athena gave her name to the Greek capital. What is it?
- On which island are the Ruins of Knossos?
- The walled town of Dubrovnik looks over which sea?
- Where can you see a Roman Amphitheatre?
- In which city is the Cathedral of St Vitus?
- Can you find a mountain range in Romania?
- The capital of Slovakia has its own castle. What is its name?
- Where are Skoda cars made?
- Name a monastery in Bulgaria.

NORTHERN EURASIA

THIS REGION SPANS two continents, Europe and Asia, separated by the Ural Mountains. Asia is bigger than Europe, taking up about 75 per cent of the land area, but only about 35 per cent of the people live there.

In the east lies Siberia, much of which is uninhabited wilderness. The climate there is extremely cold, and in winter the temperature falls below -45°C (-49°F), but this area is rich in gems and oil.

From 1922 to 1991, northern Eurasia was one vast country, called the Union of Soviet Socialist Republics, or USSR. The world's largest country, it was made up of 15 republics, each with a communist government. In 1991, the USSR split apart and all the republics became independent. The largest – the Russian Federation – remained dominant and drew many of the new nations into a Commonwealth of Independent States.

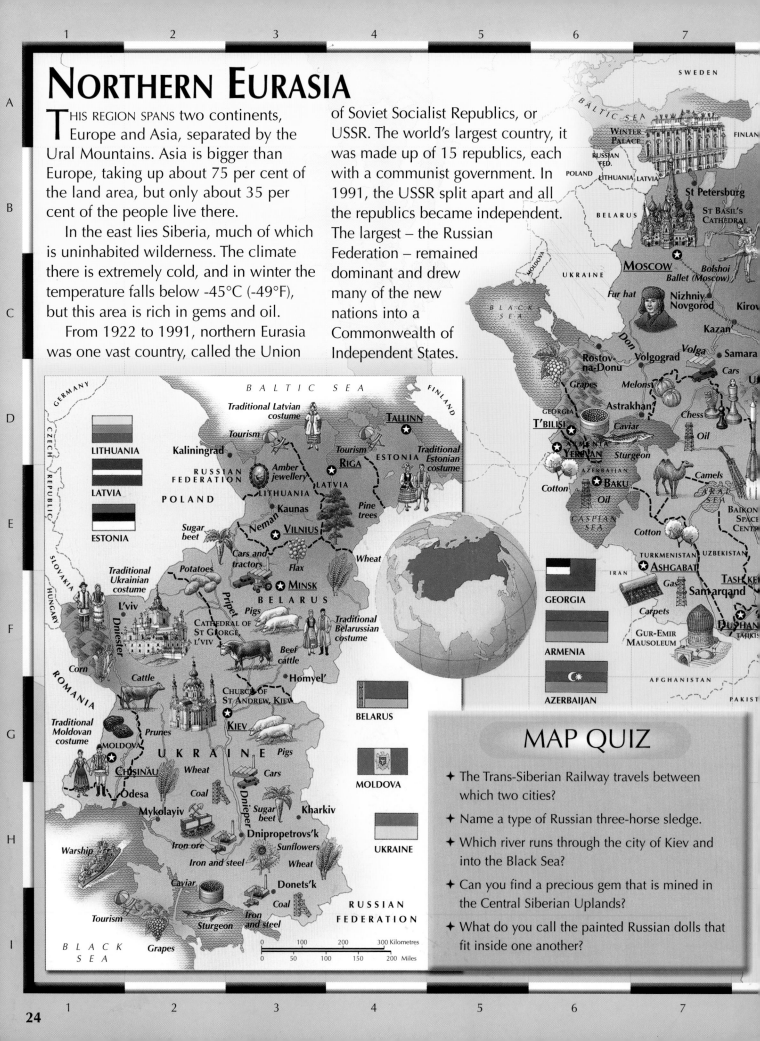

SWEDEN
BALTIC SEA
Winter Palace
FINLAN
RUSSIAN FED.
POLAND
LITHUANIA LATVIA
St Petersburg
BELARUS
St Basil's Cathedral
MOLDOVA
MOSCOW
Bolshoi Ballet (Moscow)
UKRAINE
Fur hat
Nizhniy Novgorod
Kirov
BLACK SEA
Kazan
Don
Rostov-na-Donu
Volgograd
Volga
Samara
Grapes
Melons
Cars
Astrakhan
Chess
GEORGIA
T'BILISI
Caviar
Oil
ARMENIA
YEREVAN
Sturgeon
AZERBAIJAN
Camels
Cotton
BAKU
Oil
ARAL SEA
BAIKON SPACE CENTR
CASPIAN SEA
Cotton
TURKMENISTAN UZBEKISTAN
IRAN
ASHGABAT
Gas
TASHKE
Samarqand
Carpets
GUR-EMIR MAUSOLEUM
USHAN
TAJIKIS
AFGHANISTAN
PAKIST

GERMANY
CZECH REPUBLIC
SLOVAKIA
HUNGARY
ROMANIA
BALTIC SEA
FINLAND

LITHUANIA
LATVIA
ESTONIA

Traditional Latvian costume
Tourism
TALLINN
Kaliningrad
RUSSIAN FEDERATION
Tourism
RIGA
ESTONIA
Traditional Estonian costume
POLAND
Amber jewellery
LATVIA
LITHUANIA
Kaunas
Pine trees
Sugar beet
Neman
VILNIUS
Wheat
Traditional Ukrainian costume
Cars and tractors
Flax
Potatoes
Pripet
MINSK
BELARUS
L'viv
Pigs
Traditional Belarussian costume
CATHEDRAL OF ST GEORGE, L'VIV
Pigs
Dniester
Corn
Beef cattle
Cattle
Homyel'
Traditional Moldovan costume
Prunes
CHURCH OF ST ANDREW, KIEV
MOLDOVA
KIEV
Pigs
U K R A I N E
CHIŞINĂU
Wheat
Cars
Odesa
Coal
Dnieper
Mykolayiv
Sugar beet
Kharkiv
Iron ore
Dnipropetrovs'k
Warship
Iron and steel
Sunflowers
Wheat
Caviar
Donets'k
Tourism
Coal
Sturgeon
Iron and steel
Grapes
RUSSIAN FEDERATION
BLACK SEA

0   100   200   300 Kilometres
0   50   100   150   200 Miles

GEORGIA
ARMENIA
AZERBAIJAN
BELARUS
MOLDOVA
UKRAINE

MAP QUIZ

+ The Trans-Siberian Railway travels between which two cities?

+ Name a type of Russian three-horse sledge.

+ Which river runs through the city of Kiev and into the Black Sea?

+ Can you find a precious gem that is mined in the Central Siberian Uplands?

+ What do you call the painted Russian dolls that fit inside one another?

Map labels:

9 10 11 12 13 15

BERING STRAIT

BARENTS SEA · FRANZ JOSEF LAND · Icebreaker · mansk

ARCTIC OCEAN

Gold · OSTROV VRANGELYA · BERING SEA

0 250 500 750 1000 1250 Kilometres
0 150 300 450 600 750 Miles

Harp seals · SEVERNAYA ZEMLYA · KARA SEA · NOVOSIBIRSKIYE OSTROVA · Grey whales · Chukchi tribesman

Polar bear · NOVAYA ZEMLYA · Brent geese · Walruses · Reindeer

Pine trees · Barnacle goose · Oil · Nenets tribesman · LAPTEV SEA · Yana · Indigirka · Kolyma · Furs · EAST SIBERIAN UPLANDS · Coal · Salmon

Troika (horsedrawn sledge) · Gas · Ob · Yenisey · Wolves · Furs · Lena · Yakut tribesman · Gold · Gold · Magadan · Petropavlovsk-Kamchatskiy · Fish-packing

RUSSIAN FEDERATION · Elk · Coal · Yakutsk · Spruce trees · SEA OF OKHOTSK

Fish-packing · Timber · WEST SIBERIAN LOWLANDS · Brown bears · CENTRAL SIBERIAN UPLANDS · Larch trees · KURIL ISLANDS

katerinburg · helyabinsk · Oil · Oil · Fir trees · Diamonds · Furs · Salmon · Fish-packing

Matrioshka dolls · Irtysh · Ob · Yenisey · Iron ore · TRANS-SIBERIAN RAILWAY · Manchurian tiger · Paper mills

Petropavlovsk · Omsk · Novosibirsk · Krasnoyarsk · Gold · Khabarovsk

ASTANA · Wheat · Fish-packing · LAKE BAIKAL · Irkutsk

Karaganda · Machinery and textiles · Cattle · ALTAI MTS · Fish-packing

Iron and steel · LAKE BALKHASH · Strip-mining coal · Paper mills · Vladivostok

BISHKEK · Almaty · MONGOLIA · CHINA · NORTH KOREA · SEA OF JAPAN · JAPAN

YRGYZSTAN · SOUTH KOREA

KAZAKHSTAN · TURKMENISTAN · UZBEKISTAN · TAJIKISTAN · KYRGYZSTAN · RUSSIAN FEDERATION

FACTS AND FIGURES

Largest lake:
Caspian Sea (the largest lake in the world) covers an area of 3,600,000 sq km (143,205 sq miles).
World's longest railway:
Trans-Siberian, Moscow to Nakhodka near Vladivostok, 9,438 km (5,864 miles).

ARMENIA
Capital: Yerevan
Area: 29,800 sq km (11,490 sq miles)
Population: 3,500,000
Languages: Armenian, Russian

AZERBAIJAN
Capital: Baku
Area: 86,600 sq km (33,340 sq miles)
Population: 7,700,000
Language: Azerbaijani

BELARUS
Capital: Minsk
Area: 207,600 sq km (80,134 sq miles)
Population: 10,300,000
Languages: Belarussian, Russian

ESTONIA
Capital: Tallinn
Area: 45,100 sq km (17,413 sq miles)
Population: 1,400,000
Language: Estonian

GEORGIA
Capital: T'bilisi
Area: 69,700 sq km (26,900 sq miles)
Population: 5,000,000
Language: Georgian

KAZAKHSTAN
Capital: Astana
Area: 2,717,300 sq km (1,049,155 sq miles)
Population: 16,200,000
Languages: Kazakh, Russian

KYRGYZSTAN
Capital: Bishkek
Area: 198,500 sq km (76,640 sq miles)
Population: 4,700,000
Languages: Kyrgyz, Russian

LATVIA
Capital: Riga
Area: 63,700 sq km (24,595 sq miles)
Population: 2,400,000
Languages: Latvian, Russian

LITHUANIA
Capital: Vilnius
Area: 65,200 sq km (25,170 sq miles)
Population: 3,700,000
Language: Lithuanian

MOLDOVA
Capital: Chisinau
Area: 33,700 sq km (13,000 sq miles)
Population: 4,400,000
Languages: Romanian, Moldovan

RUSSIAN FEDERATION
Capital: Moscow
Area: 17,075,000 sq km (6,592,637 sq miles)
Population: 147,000,000
Language: Russian

TAJIKISTAN
Capital: Dushanbe
Area: 143,100 sq km (55,240 sq miles)
Population: 6,200,000
Languages: Tajik, Russian

TURKMENISTAN
Capital: Ashgabat
Area: 488,100 sq km (188,455 sq miles)
Population: 4,500,000
Languages: Turkmen, Russian

UKRAINE
Capital: Kiev
Area: 603,700 sq km (231,990 sq miles)
Population: 50,700,000
Languages: Ukrainian, Russian

UZBEKISTAN
Capital: Tashkent
Area: 447,400 sq km (172,741 sq miles)
Population: 24,300,000
Languages: Uzbek, Russian

UNITED STATES AND CANADA

THE COUNTRIES THAT FORM North America are two of the largest and richest in the world; Canada is second only to the Russian Federation in land area, yet it has only about one tenth the population of the United States, its smaller neighbour. Canada has ten provinces and three territories, while the United States is made of up 50 states plus the District of Columbia (D.C.) where Washington, the capital, is located.

The original inhabitants of North America were once called 'Indians'; Canadian tribes are now more correctly known as 'First Nation' people, and those of the U.S. as 'Native Americans'. Similarly, the term 'Eskimo', previously used for natives of the far north, has been replaced by 'Inuit'. Today, the population of both countries is a mix of racial backgrounds: European, African, Asian, and Hispanic (Spanish speaking) from Central and South America.

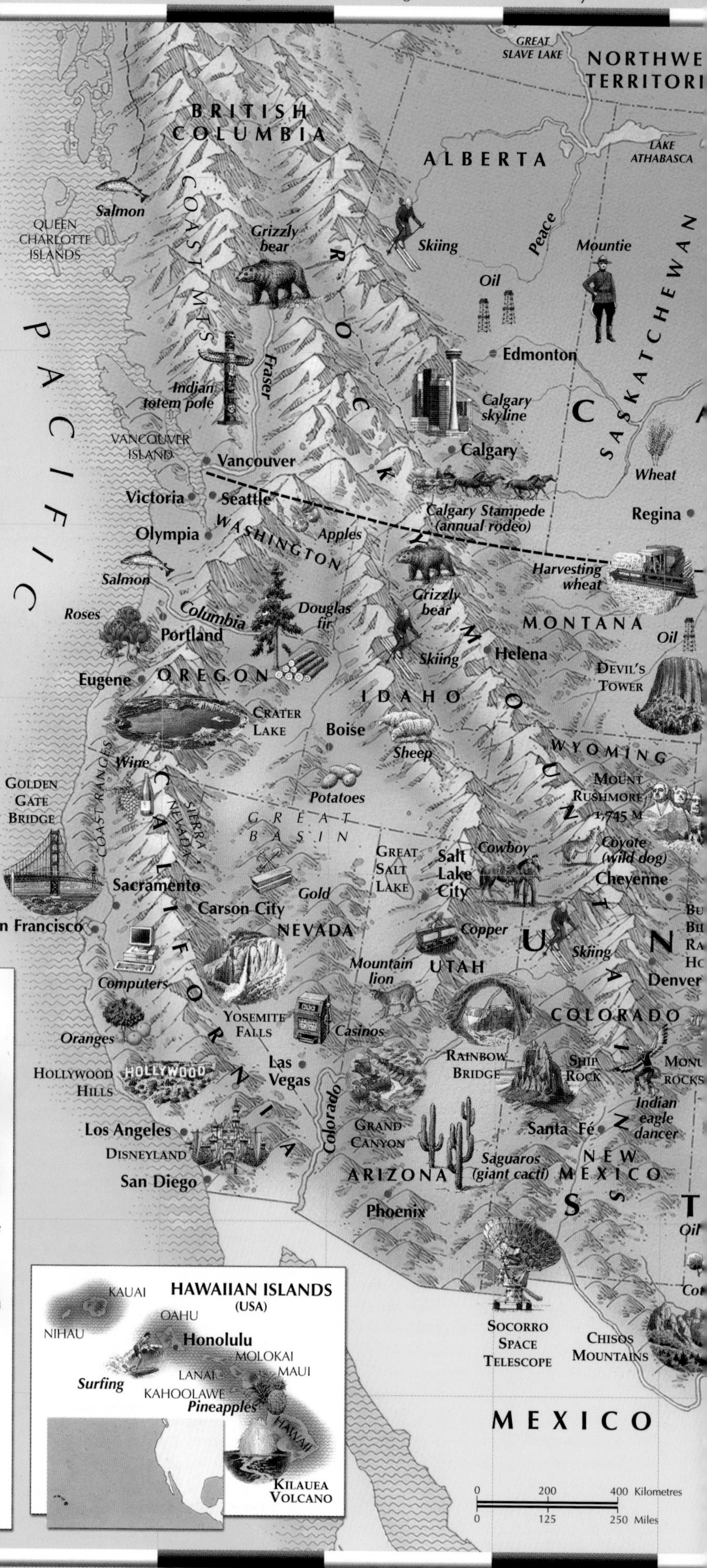

Main map labels

GREAT SLAVE LAKE
NORTHWEST TERRITORI
BRITISH COLUMBIA
ALBERTA
LAKE ATHABASCA
Salmon
Grizzly bear
Skiing
Peace
Mountie
Oil
QUEEN CHARLOTTE ISLANDS
Edmonton
Calgary skyline
SASKATCHEWAN
Fraser
Calgary
Indian totem pole
VANCOUVER ISLAND
Vancouver
Wheat
Victoria
Seattle
Calgary Stampede (annual rodeo)
Regina
Olympia
WASHINGTON
Apples
Harvesting wheat
Salmon
Columbia
Douglas fir
Grizzly bear
MONTANA
Roses
Portland
Skiing
Helena
Oil
Eugene
OREGON
DEVIL'S TOWER
CRATER LAKE
Boise
IDAHO
Wine
Sheep
WYOMING
GOLDEN GATE BRIDGE
Potatoes
MOUNT RUSHMORE 1,745 M
GREAT BASIN
Coyote (wild dog)
SIERRA NEVADA
GREAT SALT LAKE
Salt Lake City
Cowboy
Cheyenne
Sacramento
Gold
Copper
Bu Bu Ra Ho
Carson City
NEVADA
UTAH
Skiing
Mountain lion
Denver
COLORADO
San Francisco
Computers
YOSEMITE FALLS
Casinos
RAINBOW BRIDGE
SHIP ROCK
MONU ROCKS
Oranges
Las Vegas
Indian eagle dancer
HOLLYWOOD HILLS
HOLLYWOOD
Colorado
GRAND CANYON
Santa Fé
NEW MEXICO
Los Angeles
DISNEYLAND
Saguaros (giant cacti)
S
San Diego
ARIZONA
Phoenix
Oil
Co
Socorro Space Telescope
CHISOS MOUNTAINS
MEXICO
COAST RANGES
CALIFORNIA

Inset map (top left)

RUSSIAN FEDERATION
BERING SEA
BERING STRAIT
ARCTIC OCEAN
ALASKA (USA)
BEAUFORT SEA
GREENLAND (DENMARK)
PACIFIC OCEAN
CANADA
DAVIS STRAIT
LABRADOR SEA
UNITED STATES
ATLANTIC OCEAN
MEXICO
GULF OF MEXICO

Inset map (Hawaii)

HAWAIIAN ISLANDS (USA)
KAUAI
OAHU
NIHAU
Honolulu
MOLOKAI
MAUI
Surfing
LANAI
KAHOOLAWE
Pineapples
HAWAII
KILAUEA VOLCANO

PACIFIC OCEAN

0   200   400 Kilometres
0   125   250 Miles

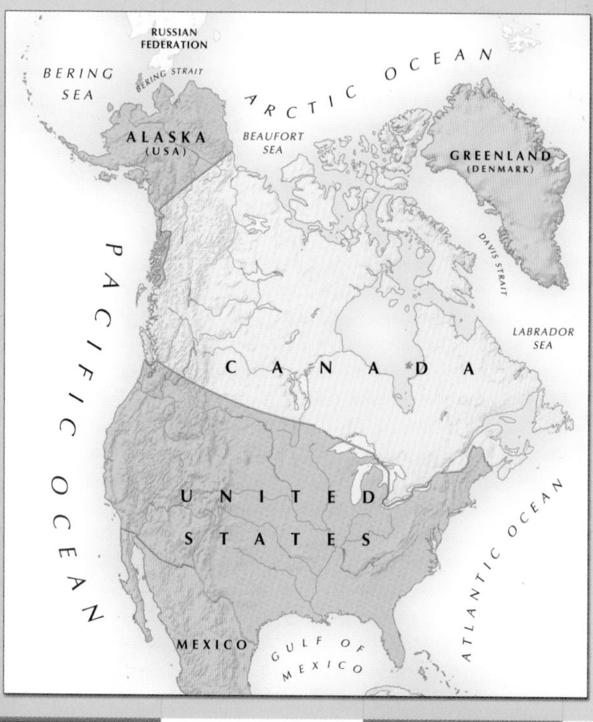

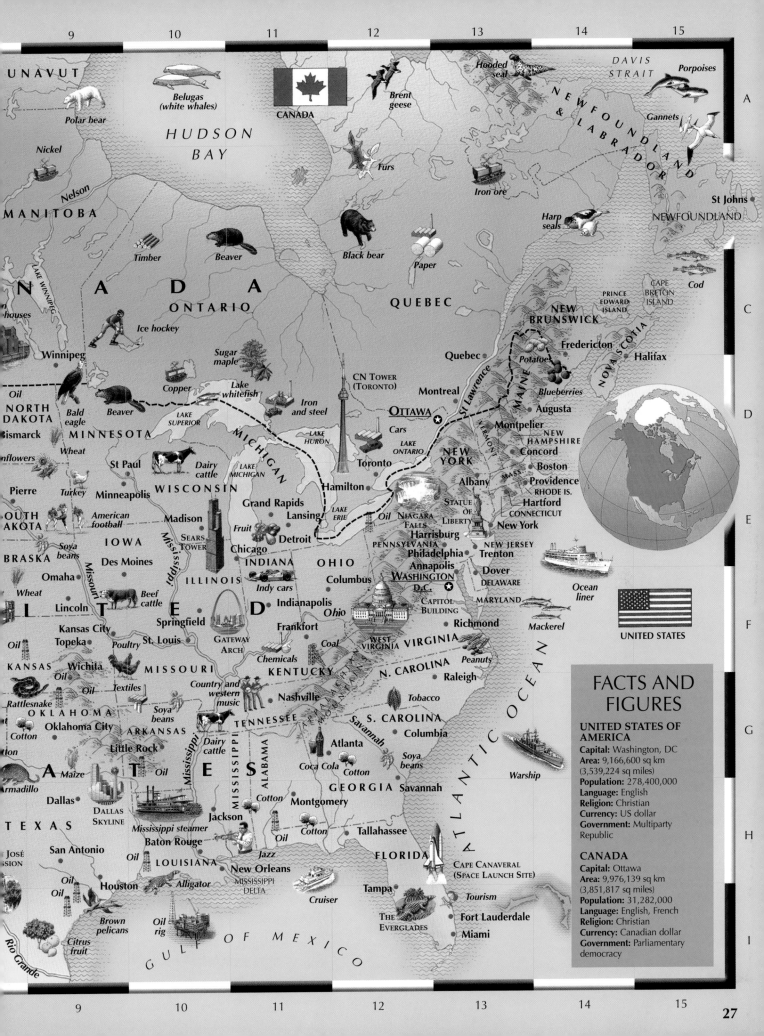

MEXICO AND CENTRAL AMERICA

CENTRAL AMERICA IS a land bridge joining the continents of North and South America. At its narrowest point, in Panama, a canal 82 km (51 miles) long links the Atlantic and Pacific oceans. There are seven countries in Central America. To the north lies Mexico and to the east lie the islands of the Caribbean, which are often called the West Indies. In the Caribbean, local poverty and tourist luxury exist side by side.

During the 16th century, the islands were settled by Europeans, who shipped black slaves from Africa to work on the farms. Today the population is a mixture of many peoples. The main languages are English, Spanish, and dialects called patois: mixtures of African languages with French or English.

There are great contrasts in the area's climate and vegetation, from the Mexican desert in the north to the southern rainforests and the coral islands in the east. Sometimes tropical storms called hurricanes rage through the Caribbean, their high winds and huge waves causing devastating damage.

Map labels

Tijuana
Mexicali
Cotton
Gila monster
LOWER CALIFORNIA
Copper
Ciudad Juárez
Saguaro cactus
GULF OF CALIFORNIA
Hermosillo
Armadillo
Elephant seal
Cattle
Rattlesnake
Chihuahua
Pack donkey
Rio Grande
MEXICO
U S A
Rice
Silver
MEXICO
Grey whales
Gold
Torreón
Boojum tree
Monterrey
Saltillo
Iron and steel
GULF OF MEXICO
Sardines
Anchovies
Tuna
Brown pelicans
Monarch butterfly
Citrus fruit
Flamingos
Shrimps
Folk dancers
Lobster
PACIFIC OCEAN
Huichol Indian
Oil
Tourism
Grapes
Shrimps
CHICHÉN ITZÁ (MAYA CITY)
Tourism
Aguascalientes
Tampico
León
NATIONAL CATHEDRAL (MEXICO CITY)
Guadalajara
Scarlet macaw
Swordfish
Oil
Oil
Tequila
MEXICO CITY
Veracruz
TIKAL (MAYA CITY)
Fisherman on Lake Pátzcuaro
Puebla
Belize City
POPOCATÉPETL VOLCANO 5,452 m
Tzeltal Indian
BELMOPAN
Tourism
OLMEC HEAD
Acapulco
GUATEMALA
Aztec god
GUATEMALA CITY
Quetzal
Coffee
Banana
Shrimps
SAN SALVADOR
EL SALVADOR

MAP QUIZ

- ✦ In what country would you find a gila monster?
- ✦ Which Caribbean islands are famous for steel bands?
- ✦ Name the volcano that lies close to Mexico City.
- ✦ Where would you go to buy world-famous cigars?
- ✦ In what country is the ancient Mayan city of Tikal?
- ✦ In which island country was reggae music born?

Flags

GUATEMALA BELIZE HONDURAS

EL SALVADOR NICARAGUA COSTA RICA PANAMA

FACTS AND FIGURES

Jamaica ("island of springs") is a popular tourist resort.

CUBA
Capital: Havana

DOMINICA
Capital: Roseau

DOMINICAN REPUBLIC
Capital: Santo Domingo

EL SALVADOR
Capital: San Salvador

GRENADA
Capital: St George's

GUADELOUPE
Capital: Basse Terre

GUATEMALA
Capital: Guatemala City

HAITI
Capital: Port-au-Prince

HONDURAS
Capital: Tegucigalpa

JAMAICA
Capital: Kingston

ANTIGUA & BARBUDA
Capital: St John's

ARUBA
Capital: Oranjestad

BAHAMAS
Capital: Nassau

BARBADOS
Capital: Bridgetown

BELIZE
Capital: Belmopan

COSTA RICA
Capital: San José

MARTINIQUE
Capital: Fort-de-France

MEXICO
Capital: Mexico City

NETHERLANDS ANTILLES
Capital: Willemstad

NICARAGUA
Capital: Managua

PANAMA
Capital: Panama City

PUERTO RICO
Capital: San Juan

ST KITTS & NEVIS
Capital: Basseterre

ST LUCIA
Capital: Castries

ST VINCENT & THE GRENADINES
Capital: Kingstown

TRINIDAD & TOBAGO
Capital: Port-of-Spain

DOMINICA

ST LUCIA

ST KITTS & NEVIS

ANTIGUA & BARBUDA

BAHAMAS

ST VINCENT & THE GRENADINES

BARBADOS

GRENADA

TRINIDAD & TOBAGO

CUBA

JAMAICA

HAITI

DOMINICAN REPUBLIC

Map labels

ATLANTIC OCEAN

U S A

Tourism

B A H A M A S

Nassau

STRAITS OF FLORIDA

Scuba diver

Sugar cane

Cruise liner

Coral reefs

TURKS & CAICOS ISLANDS (UK)

Cocoa

Coral reefs

Tourism

Frigate bird

ANGUILLA (UK)

ANTIGUA & BARBUDA

Havana

HAVANA

C U B A

Pineapples

Coffee

HAITI

DOMINICAN REPUBLIC

SANTO DOMINGO

VIRGIN ISLANDS (USA/UK)

ST KITTS & NEVIS

GUADELOUPE (Fr)

PUERTO RICO (US)

SAN JUAN

MONTSERRAT (UK)

Cigars

PORT-AU-PRINCE

Coconuts

DOMINICA

Scuba diver

CAYMAN ISLANDS (UK)

JAMAICA

KINGSTON

Sharks

Sailing

MARTINIQUE (Fr)

ST LUCIA

BARBADOS

Green turtle

Reggae music

Rum

ST VINCENT & THE GRENADINES

Nutmeg and mace

Grapefruit

GRENADA

C A R I B B E A N   S E A

Steel bands

HONDURAS

Cattle

ARUBA (Neth)

TRINIDAD & TOBAGO

TEGUCIGALPA

Coffee

Bananas

PANAMA CANAL

NETHERLANDS ANTILLES (Neth)

COLOMBIA

VENEZUELA

NICARAGUA

Coffee

MANAGUA

SAN JOSÉ

COSTA RICA

P A N A M A

PANAMA CITY

Spider monkey

Toucan

| 0 | 200 | 400 | 600 | 800 Kilometres |
| 0 | 100 | 200 | 300 | 400 | 500 Miles |

South America

THE CONTINENT of South America is dominated by the snow-capped Andes mountains and the wide Amazon river, which flows through the vast rainforests of the north. South of the Amazon are the grassy plains of the Pampas and vast expanses of barren, windswept desert. South America's wealth comes from agriculture, tourism and the export of beef. Natural resources such as coal, copper, gold, iron ore, lead, natural gas, oil and tin also contribute.

During the 16th century, the land was settled by Europeans, who conquered many of the native peoples. Among these were the Incas, whose civilization flourished in the Peruvian Andes until it was destroyed in 1532-33 by Spanish conquistadors.

URUGUAY
SURINAM
VENEZUELA
PERU
GUYANA
COLOMBIA
BRAZIL
BOLIVIA
ECUADOR
PARAGUAY
ARGENTINA
CHILE

ATLANTIC OCEAN
PACIFIC

BRAZIL
GUYANA
VENEZUELA
COLOMBIA
ECUADOR
PERU
SURINAM
FRENCH GUIANA (France)
PANAMA
ANDES MTS

Natal
Recife
Church of Our Lady of Carmo
Cocoa
Fortaleza
Bananas
Teresina
Brazil nuts
Belém
Mango tree
MARAJÓ ISLAND
Brasília Cathedral Dome
Tocantins
Araguaia
Kayapo Indian
Gold
Xingu
Suya Indian
Jangada fishing raft
Lobster
Green turtle
Water buffalo
Quito
Gold and blue macaw
CAYENNE
ARIANE ROCKET LAUNCH SITE
PARAMARIBO
GEORGETOWN
Wayana Indian
Anaconda
Caiman
Amazon
MANAUS OPERA HOUSE
Manaus
Humming bird
Umbrella bird
Porto Velho
Negro
Capybara (world's largest rodent)
Rainforest
Purus
Madeira
Two-toed sloth
Rubber trees
Angel Falls
Red howler monkey
Indian hunter
Toco toucan
MACHU PICCHU (Inca City)
Ciudad Bolívar
Diamonds
Scarlet ibis
CARACAS
Valencia
Barquisimeto
Harpy eagle
Orinoco
Jaguar
Peruvian cock-of-the-rock
Iquitos
Llama
Pre-Columbian stone idol
BOGOTÁ
BOGOTÁ CATHEDRAL
Barranquilla
Cartagena
Medellín
Manizales
Cali
Emeralds
Bananas
COTOPAXI 5,897 m
Cavies (guinea pigs)
Indian flute players
Coffee
Piura
Chiclayo
Trujillo
HUASCARÁN 6,768 m
LIMA

30

MAP QUIZ

◆ In what type of ranching would a gaucho be employed?

◆ What is the name of the ancient Inca city in Peru?

◆ Which capital city features a dramatic domed cathedral?

◆ West of the Andes mountains, in northern Chile, is a huge desert. What is it called?

◆ In which country is the Ariane Rocket Launch Site?

◆ What is a carreta?

◆ Lake Titicaca is the highest navigable lake in the world. Where is it?

◆ Sugar Loaf Mountain stands at the entrance to a famous South American harbour city. Which one is it?

FACTS AND FIGURES

Highest mountains:
Mt Aconcagua (Argentina), 6,959 m (22,831 ft); Ojos del Salado (Argentina-Chile), 6,880 m (22,572 ft); Huascarán (Peru), 6,768 m (22,205 ft); Illimani (Bolivia), 6,402 m (21,004 ft).

Longest rivers:
Amazon, 6,437 km (4,000 miles); Paraná, 4,500 km (2,796 miles); Madeira, 3,199 km (1,988 miles); São Francisco, 3,199 km (1,988 miles); Purús, 2,993 km (1,860 miles).

Largest lake:
Lake Titicaca (Peru-Bolivia), 8,340 sq km (3,220 sq miles).

World's highest waterfall:
Angel Falls (Venezuela), 979 m (3,212 ft).

Largest cities:
São Paulo (Brazil), 15,199,500; Buenos Aires (Argentina), 9,927,400; Rio de Janeiro (Brazil), 9,600,600; Lima (Peru), 6,483,900; Santiago (Chile), 5,170,300.

World's leading coffee grower:
Brazil grows around 4,000,000 tonnes (3,936,826 tons) of coffee each year.

GALAPAGOS ISLANDS (ECUADOR)

Galapagos giant tortoise

Marine iguana

ISABELA ISLAND

0 100 200 Kilometres
0 75 150 Miles

FALKLAND ISLANDS (UK)

Albatross

★ STANLEY

Sheep

Rock hopper penguins

Hake

0 50 100 200 Kilometres
0 125 150 Miles

200 400 600 800 Kilometres
125 250 375 500 Miles

ATLANTIC OCEAN

Shrimps

CORCOVADO STATUE OF CHRIST (RIO DE JANEIRO)

SUGAR LOAF MT 395 M

Belo Horizonte

Rio de Janeiro

Humming bird

Carnival

Campinas

Football

São Paulo

Coffee

Cars

Curitiba

Oranges

Coffee

PORTO ALEGRE CATHEDRAL

Porto Alegre

Tobacco

BOLIVIA

Santa Cruz

Puya raimondii (world's tallest herb)

Campo Grande

MATO GROSSO

Jabiru stork

Cochabamba

★ SUCRE

Bolivian Indians

Arica

Iquique

ATACAMA DESERT

LICANCABUR VOLCANO 5,921 M

Antofagasta

ANDES

PARAGUAY

CHACO

Cotton

★ ASUNCIÓN

Concepción

Paraná

Paraguay

Corrientes

Resistencia

Maté (type of tea)

Paraná

GRAN CHACO

Carreta (ox-drawn cart)

San Miguel de Tucumán

Santiago del Estero

Salado

Santa Fe

Rosario

Paraná

Wine

San Juan

Córdoba

ARGENTINA

URUGUAY

MONTEVIDEO ★

Tourism

RIVER PLATE

BUENOS AIRES ★

La Plata

COLON OPERA HOUSE

Tango dancers

Mar del Plata

Tourism

Cherries

Mt ACONCAGUA 6,959 M

Mendoza

Ojos DEL SALADO 6,880 M

SANTIAGO ★

Rancagua

Viña del Mar

Valparaíso ★

Concepción

Mackerel

Gaucho (cattleherder)

PAMPAS

Colorado

Negro

Maned wolf

Atuel

Darwin's rhea

Huaso (Chilean cowboy)

Trout

Salmon

Timber

Chubut

Chico

Oil

Comodoro Rivadavia

Sealions

CHILE

PATAGONIA

Right whale

Bahía Blanca

Tourism

Sheep

Oil

Rio Gallegos

MORENO GLACIER

Fur seals

Punta Arenas

STRAIT OF MAGELLAN

TIERRA DEL FUEGO

Ushuaia

CAPE HORN

ATLANTIC OCEAN

Dusky dolphins

THE MIDDLE EAST

THE MIDDLE EAST (also known as southwest Asia) lies at the join of three continents – Asia, Africa, and Europe – and takes in many different landscapes. There is a wide variety too, in cultures and religions, and these differences have resulted in longstanding political instability in the region.

The countries surrounding the Mediterranean are wetter than the others, and crops such as citrus fruits, olives and wheat are grown there. To the south stretch the huge deserts of Saudi Arabia. Earlier this century, the world's largest deposits of oil were discovered in the countries around the Gulf, and the oil-fields in the region now supply the world.

Some of the world's first settled farming communities grew up in the Fertile Crescent, which stretches from the Mediterranean to the area between the Tigris and Euphrates rivers. Of great historical interest, too, is the city of Jerusalem, which is a holy place for Christians, Muslims and Jews, visited by millions of people each year.

MAP QUIZ

- ✦ An old Syrian city gives its name to a luxurious textile weave. What is it?

- ✦ The ancient city of Baghdad lies on what river?

- ✦ Which sea is known for its caviar-producing sturgeon?

- ✦ What is a traditional Arab sailing boat called?

- ✦ From which tree does the biblical perfume called Frankincense come?

- ✦ A country in this region has the same name as its capital city. Which one is it?

- ✦ What mountain range borders the Gulf in Iran?

- ✦ On which sea does the city of Jedda lie?

- ✦ Can you find two textile fibres that are produced in the Middle East?

- ✦ Muslim women cover their faces in public. What is the name of the veil they wear?

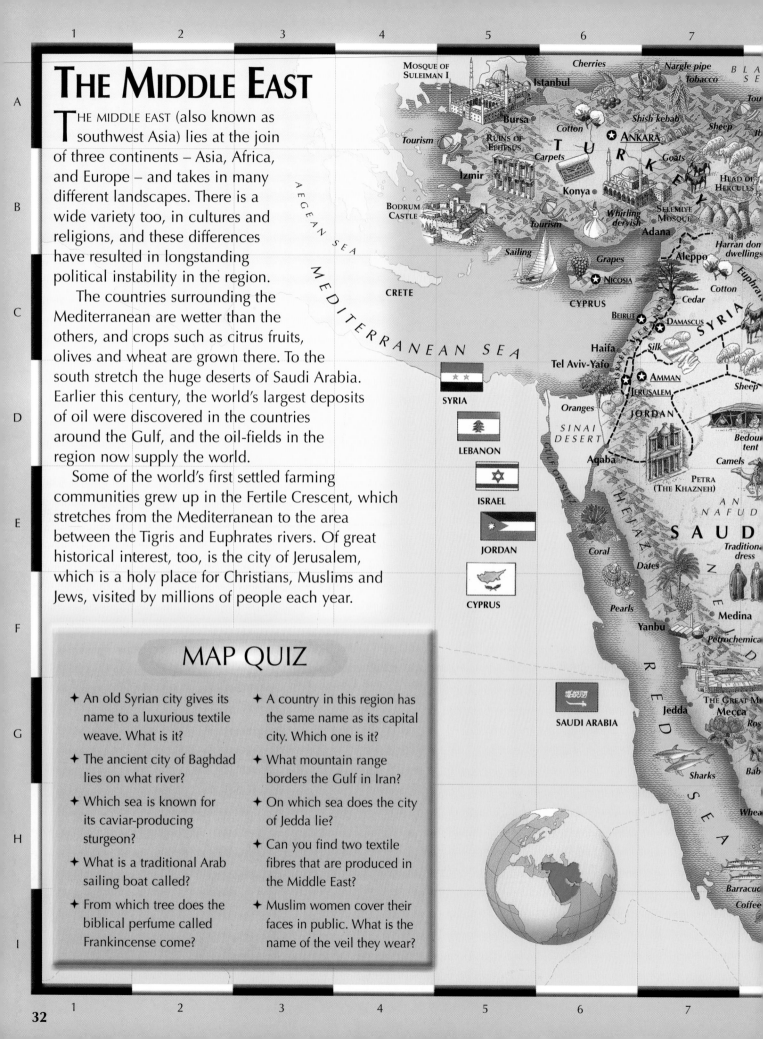

SYRIA

LEBANON

ISRAEL

JORDAN

CYPRUS

SAUDI ARABIA

GEORGIA
Tea
ARMENIA
Bears
Tobacco
LAKE VAN
MT. ARARAT 5,137 m
Apples
Melons
Tabriz
Kurdish dress
AZERBAIJAN
CASPIAN SEA
Tea
Rice
Sturgeon
Caviar
TURKMENISTAN
Mashhad
Turquoise
ELBURZ MTS
Silk
Carpets
☪ TEHRAN
LAKE NAMAK
THE ROYAL MOSQUE
Traditional dress
Pigeon towers
Cotton
Mosul
Oil
HAYDAR KHANAH MOSQUE
Dates
Qom
Bakhtaran
Esfahan
IRAN
AFGHANISTAN
GHDAD ★
AQ
Tigris
ZIGGURAT AT UR
Arab marsh reed house
Oil
Ahvaz
Chemicals
Oil
Textiles
Oil
PERSEPOLIS (PALACE STAIRCASE)
Goats
Basra
Abadan
Oil
Shiraz
ZAGROS MOUNTAINS
Sheep
PAKISTAN
Cattle
KUWAIT
Oil
Oil
Petrochemicals
Oil
Gas
Gas
BAM
ARABIA
Al Jubayl
THE GULF
Oil
Oil tanker
Yashmak (face veil)
Oil
BAHRAIN
MANAMA
STRAIT OF HORMUZ
AD DAHNA
QATAR
Oil
RIYADH ★
DOHA
Oil
ABU DHABI
Dubai
Sardines
GULF OF OMAN
Oil
Arab horses
Falconry
Oil
UNITED ARAB EMIRATES
Dates
MUSCAT
Dhow (Arab boat)
ARABIAN DESERT
Khanjar (Arab dagger)
Oil
Oil
Incense burner
Sand dunes 213 m
JIZAN DAM
AR RUB' AL KHALI
Kummas Omani (embroidered cap)
OMAN
ARABIAN SEA
Ancient painted house
Arabian oryx
Oil tanker
Camels
Frankincense (Boswellia tree)
YEMEN
SANA ★
Dates
Dhow (Arab boat)
Cotton
Aden

0 150 300 450 600 Kilometres
0 100 200 300 400 Miles

TURKEY
IRAQ
IRAN

OMAN
KUWAIT
BAHRAIN
YEMEN
QATAR
UNITED ARAB EMIRATES
Dhow (Arab boat)

FACTS AND FIGURES

Dhow (Arab boat) off the Yemen coast.

Largest city:
Tehran (Iran), 8,712,100.

Hottest capital:
Riyadh, Saudi Arabia, is the hottest capital city in the world, with average July temperatures of over 40°C (104°F).

Dunes are formed when desert winds blow the sand into mounds.

BAHRAIN
Capital: Manama
Area: 678 sq km (262 sq miles)

CYPRUS
Capital: Nicosia
Area: 9,251 sq km (3,571 sq miles)

IRAN
Capital: Tehran
Area: 1,648,000 sq km (636,297 sq miles)

IRAQ
Capital: Baghdad
Area: 438,317 sq km (169,235 sq miles)

ISRAEL
Capital: Jerusalem
Area: 20,770 sq km (8,017 sq miles) plus the Golan Heights and West Bank, total area 7,418 sq km (2,864 sq miles)

JORDAN
Capital: Amman
Area: 89,206 sq km (34,443 sq miles)

KUWAIT
Capital: Kuwait
Area: 17,818 sq km (6,879 sq miles)

LEBANON
Capital: Beirut
Area: 10,400 sq km (4,015 sq miles)

OMAN
Capital: Muscat
Area: 212,457 sq km (82,030 sq miles)

QATAR
Capital: Doha
Area: 11,000 sq km (4,247 sq miles)

SAUDI ARABIA
Capital: Riyadh
Area: 2,149,690 sq km (830,001 sq miles)

SYRIA
Capital: Damascus
Area: 185,180 sq km (71,500 sq miles)

TURKEY
Capital: Ankara
Area: 779,452 sq km (300,948 sq miles)

UNITED ARAB EMIRATES
Capital: Abu Dhabi
Area: 83,600 sq km (32,278 sq miles)

YEMEN
Capital: Sana
Area: 527,968 sq km (203,850 sq miles)

SOUTHERN ASIA

THE LARGEST COUNTRY in Southern Asia is India, and the region is often called the "Indian subcontinent". Over one billion people live there – about 22 per cent of the world's population. Most people live in the fertile river and coastal plains. Nearly three-quarters are farmers, who depend heavily on seasonal rains. The most important crop is rice.

India was united in the 16th and 17th centuries under Mogul rule. In the 18th century, it became part of the British Empire, but gained independence in 1947, when it was divided into two: Hindu India and Muslim Pakistan. In 1971, east Pakistan became a separate country, Bangladesh.

Today, Pakistan and India are industrial nations. Pakistan's industries include food processing, textiles and chemicals. India produces oil, coal, manganese, iron ore, and copper, and has iron and steel, car manufacturing, and computer industries.

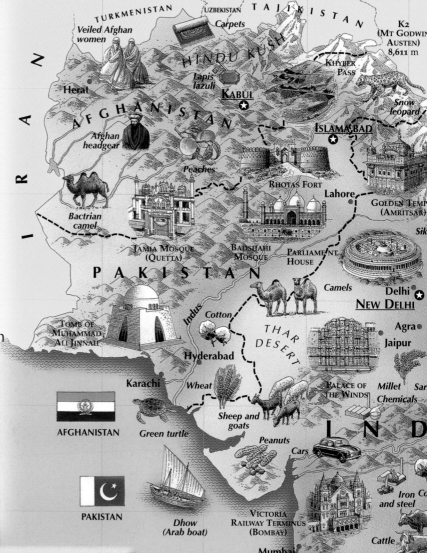

MAP QUIZ

+ Hindu people believe the Ganges River is holy. In which mountain range is its source?

+ Through what countries does the region's longest river, the Indus, flow?

+ Where could you see 'giraffe-necked' women with metal rings around their throat?

+ In which city is the huge Victoria Railway Terminus?

+ Name the traditional Indian loincloth woven from undyed, homespun cotton.

+ Can you locate the highest mountain in Southern Asia?

+ What island is famous for its thriving trade in tea?

+ Which stringed instrument, sometimes used in western music, is associated with India?

+ What two countries are linked by the Kyber Pass?

+ Where would you go to find both ruby and jade mines?

+ In Burma (Myanmar), which animal is used to haul heavy teak logs?

Mountain Peaks in the Himalayas

Mt Everest 8,848 m

Kanchenjunga 8,598 m

Makalu I 8,463 m

Dhaulagiri 8,167 m

Nanga Parbat 8,126 m

FACTS AND FIGURES

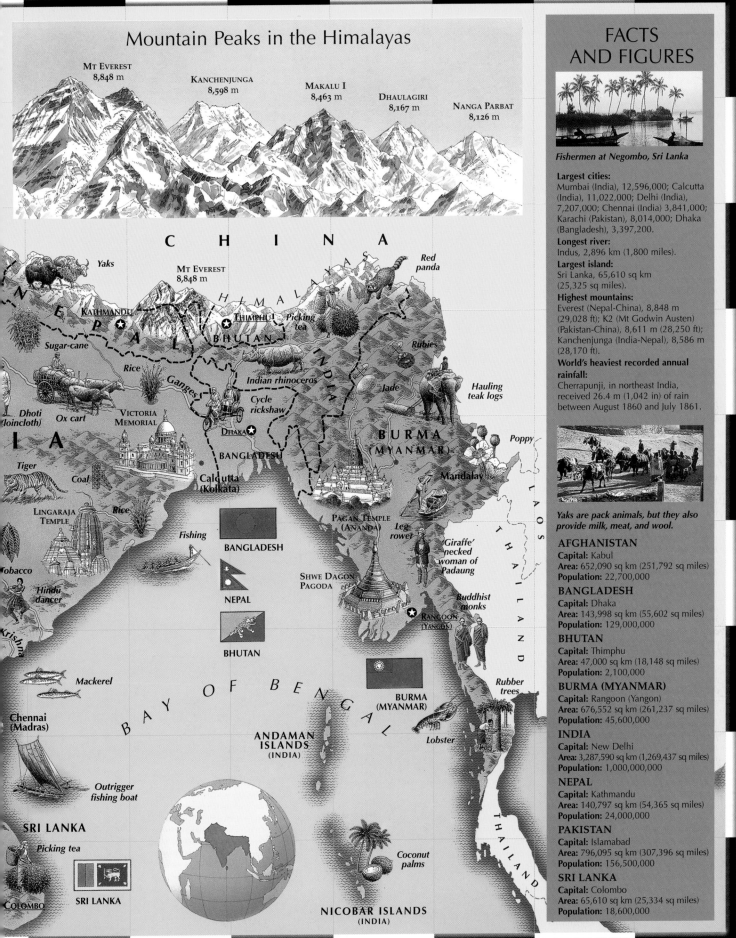

Fishermen at Negombo, Sri Lanka

Largest cities:
Mumbai (India), 12,596,000; Calcutta (India), 11,022,000; Delhi (India), 7,207,000; Chennai (India) 3,841,000; Karachi (Pakistan), 8,014,000; Dhaka (Bangladesh), 3,397,200.

Longest river:
Indus, 2,896 km (1,800 miles).

Largest island:
Sri Lanka, 65,610 sq km (25,325 sq miles).

Highest mountains:
Everest (Nepal-China), 8,848 m (29,028 ft); K2 (Mt Godwin Austen) (Pakistan-China), 8,611 m (28,250 ft); Kanchenjunga (India-Nepal), 8,586 m (28,170 ft).

World's heaviest recorded annual rainfall:
Cherrapunji, in northeast India, received 26.4 m (1,042 in) of rain between August 1860 and July 1861.

Yaks are pack animals, but they also provide milk, meat, and wool.

AFGHANISTAN
Capital: Kabul
Area: 652,090 sq km (251,792 sq miles)
Population: 22,700,000

BANGLADESH
Capital: Dhaka
Area: 143,998 sq km (55,602 sq miles)
Population: 129,000,000

BHUTAN
Capital: Thimphu
Area: 47,000 sq km (18,148 sq miles)
Population: 2,100,000

BURMA (MYANMAR)
Capital: Rangoon (Yangon)
Area: 676,552 sq km (261,237 sq miles)
Population: 45,600,000

INDIA
Capital: New Delhi
Area: 3,287,590 sq km (1,269,437 sq miles)
Population: 1,000,000,000

NEPAL
Capital: Kathmandu
Area: 140,797 sq km (54,365 sq miles)
Population: 24,000,000

PAKISTAN
Capital: Islamabad
Area: 796,095 sq km (307,396 sq miles)
Population: 156,500,000

SRI LANKA
Capital: Colombo
Area: 65,610 sq km (25,334 sq miles)
Population: 18,600,000

Map labels:

CHINA — Yaks — Red panda — Mt Everest 8,848 m — KATHMANDU — NEPAL — THIMPHU — Picking tea — BHUTAN — HIMALAYAS — Rubies — Sugar-cane — Rice — Ganges — Indian rhinoceros — Cycle rickshaw — INDIA — Jade — Hauling teak logs — Dhoti (loincloth) — Ox cart — VICTORIA MEMORIAL — DHAKA — BANGLADESH — BURMA (MYANMAR) — Poppy — Tiger — Coal — Calcutta (Kolkata) — Mandalay — LINGARAJA TEMPLE — Rice — Fishing — BANGLADESH — PAGAN TEMPLE (ANANDA) — Leg rower — Tobacco — Hindu dancer — NEPAL — SHWE DAGON PAGODA — Giraffe' necked woman of Padaung — LAOS — THAILAND — Krishna — BHUTAN — Buddhist monks — RANGOON (YANGON) — Mackerel — BAY OF BENGAL — BURMA (MYANMAR) — Rubber trees — Chennai (Madras) — ANDAMAN ISLANDS (INDIA) — Lobster — Outrigger fishing boat — SRI LANKA — Picking tea — SRI LANKA — COLOMBO — Coconut palms — NICOBAR ISLANDS (INDIA)

JAPAN

L YING EAST OF THE MAIN PART of Asia, Japan is made up of four major islands – Hokkaido, Honshu, Shikoku, and Kyushu – and thousands of smaller ones. In this area, where two plates of the Earth's crust meet, earthquakes are common.

Nearly three-quarters of the country is mountainous and wooded, but the areas that are suitable for agriculture are cultivated very efficiently. The main crop is rice. Because so little of the land can be farmed, the Japanese eat a lot of fish, and they catch more fish than any other nation. Most of Japan's 126 million people live on a small area of flat, largely coastal, land, mainly around the great south-coast cities of Honshu island, such as Nagoya, Tokyo and Osaka.

In the last 40 years Japan has become one of the world's most important industrial nations. This is all the more remarkable because the oil and most of the raw materials that are needed in manufacturing have to be imported. Japanese cars, electrical goods, ships, cameras, and many other products are exported all over the world.

MAP QUIZ

✦ Mount Fuji, Japan's highest mountain, is located on which of the four main islands?

✦ For more than 1,000 years, the city of Kyoto was the capital of Japan. Where is Kyoto?

✦ Which style of formal wrestling originated in Japan?

✦ An important religious shrine is shown on Honshu island. What faith does it represent?

✦ What kind of food is tofu?

✦ Can you find the location of an annual snow festival?

✦ Name a type of theatre that is popular in Japan.

✦ Which gem is found in the seas around Japan?

✦ What is the name of the ancient fortified castle on the Japanese island of Shikoku?

✦ Miniature trees are highly prized in Japanese culture. What are they called?

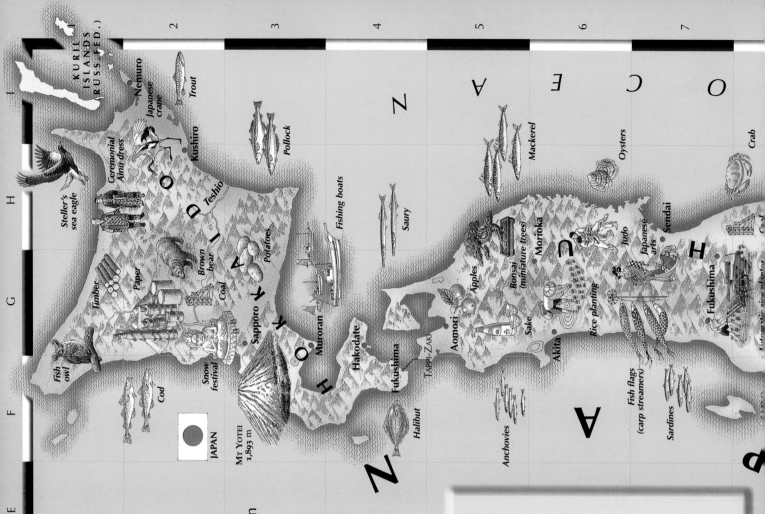

KURIL ISLANDS (RUSS. FED.)

Nemuro
Japanese crane
Trout
Kushiro
Pollock

HOKKAIDO

Ceremonial Ainu dress
Steller's sea eagle
Teshio
Timber
Paper
Brown bear
Coal
Potatoes
Fish owl
Cod
Snow festival
Sapporo
Muroran

Mt Yotei 1,893 m

JAPAN

HONSHU

Hakodate
Fukushima
Tappi-Zaki

Fishing boats
Saury
Mackerel
Oysters
Crab

Morioka
Judo
Japanese arts
Sendai
Fukushima

Bonsai (miniature trees)
Rice planting
Sake
Aomori
Apples
Akita

Halibut
Anchovies
Sardines
Fish flags (carp streamers)

JAPAN

N

FACTS AND FIGURES

Highest mountain:
Mt Fuji, 3,776 m (12,388 ft).
Main ports:
Tokyo, Yokohama, Osaka, Kobe.
Wettest area:
All of Japan has high rainfall, but the wettest place is the southernmost island of Kyushu, where average rainfall reaches over 2,200 mm (86.6 in) per year.
Coldest area:
Hokkaido has average winter temperatures of -10°C (14°F).
Longest railway tunnel in the world:
The Seikan Rail Tunnel in Japan runs for 53.85 km (33.46 miles) between the headland of Tappi-Zaki on Honshu island and the small town of Fukushima on Hokkaido (not to be confused Fukushima city on Honshu).

World's largest fishing fleet:
Japan catches around 14 per cent of the total world catch – more than any other country. Each Japanese person eats an average of 30 kg (65 lbs) of fish a year.
World's tallest lighthouse:
The steel lighthouse in Yokohama, Japan is 106 m (348 ft) high. It can be seen from 32 km (20 miles) away.
Food:
Only 15 per cent of the land, mostly on the coastal plains, can be farmed. But despite this, Japan is 70 per cent self-sufficient in food.
World's top oil importer:
Japan. The *Seawise Giant*, a Japanese tanker built in 1981, is the largest tanker in the world. It is almost 500 m (547 yards) long and can carry 565,000 tonnes of crude oil.

Largest cities:
Tokyo, 7,976,000; Yokohama, 3,233,000; Osaka, 2,506,000; Nagoya, 2,098,000; Sapporo, 1,687,000; Kyoto, 1,339,000; Kobe, 1,459,000; Fukuoka, 1,142,000.
Four largest islands:
Honshu, Hokkaido, Kyushu, Shikoku.

Tokyo, Japan's bustling capital.

JAPAN
Capital: Tokyo
Area: 377,801 sq km (145,835 sq miles)
Population: 126,700,000
Language: Japanese
Religions: Shinto, Buddhist
Currency: Yen

Temple statue at Nikko, Honshu.

A Japanese garden in Hiroshima.

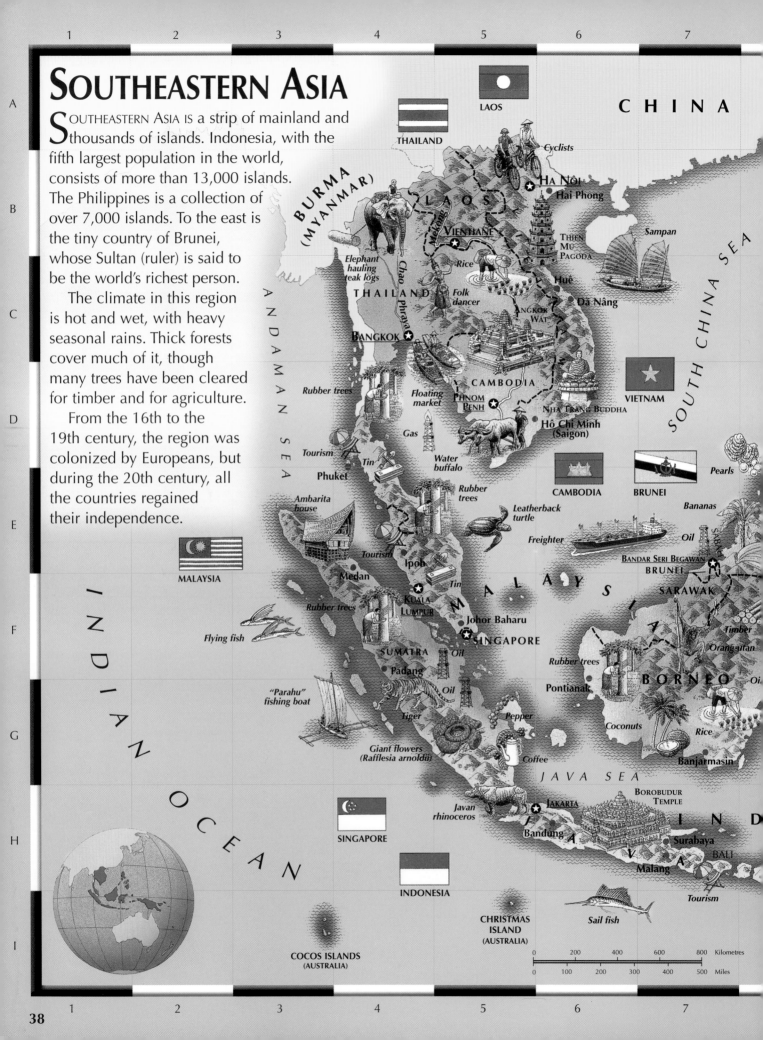

SOUTHEASTERN ASIA

SOUTHEASTERN ASIA IS a strip of mainland and thousands of islands. Indonesia, with the fifth largest population in the world, consists of more than 13,000 islands. The Philippines is a collection of over 7,000 islands. To the east is the tiny country of Brunei, whose Sultan (ruler) is said to be the world's richest person.

The climate in this region is hot and wet, with heavy seasonal rains. Thick forests cover much of it, though many trees have been cleared for timber and for agriculture.

From the 16th to the 19th century, the region was colonized by Europeans, but during the 20th century, all the countries regained their independence.

LAOS

THAILAND

CHINA

BURMA (MYANMAR)

LAOS

Cyclists

HA NÔI
Hai Phong

VIENTIANE

THIEN MU PAGODA

Sampan

Elephant hauling teak logs

Rice

Huê

THAILAND

Folk dancer

Da Nâng

ANGKOR WAT

SOUTH CHINA SEA

Chao Phraya

BANGKOK

CAMBODIA

Rubber trees

Floating market

PHNOM PENH

NHA TRANG BUDDHA

Hô Chi Minh (Saigon)

VIETNAM

Gas

Tourism

Water buffalo

CAMBODIA

BRUNEI

Pearls

Tin

Phuket

Rubber trees

Leatherback turtle

Bananas

Ambarita house

Tourism

Freighter

Oil

BANDAR SERI BEGAWAN

BRUNEI

SABAH

MALAYSIA

Ipoh

Medan

Tin

SARAWAK

Timber

Orangutan

INDIAN OCEAN

Rubber trees

KUALA LUMPUR

MALAYSIA

BORNEO

Oil

Flying fish

SUMATRA

Padang

Johor Baharu

SINGAPORE

Oil

Rubber trees

Pontianak

"Parahu" fishing boat

Tiger

Oil

Pepper

Coconuts

Rice

Giant flowers (Rafflesia arnoldii)

Coffee

Banjarmasin

JAVA SEA

SINGAPORE

Javan rhinoceros

JAKARTA

BOROBUDUR TEMPLE

IND

Bandung

JAVA

Surabaya

BALI

INDONESIA

Malang

Tourism

CHRISTMAS ISLAND (AUSTRALIA)

Sail fish

COCOS ISLANDS (AUSTRALIA)

| 0 | 200 | 400 | 600 | 800 | Kilometres |
| 0 | 100 | 200 | 300 | 400 | 500 | Miles |

A

FACTS AND FIGURES

Largest cities:
Jakarta (Indonesia), 9,000,000;
Manila (Philippines), 7,729,000;
Bangkok (Thailand), 5,875,900;
Ho Chi-Minh (Vietnam,
previously called Saigon),
4,075,700.

Highest mountain:
Puncak Jaya (Indonesia),
5,040 m (16,503 ft).

Largest island:
New Guinea, 808,510 sq km
(312,168 sq miles).

Longest river:
Mekong, 4,184 km
(2,600 miles).

Longest name in the world:
The Thai name for Bangkok
is Krungthep maha nakorn,
amarn rattanakosindra,
mahindrayudhya, mahadilok
pop noparatana rajdhani
mahasathan, amorn piman
avatarn satit, sakkatultiya
visanukarn prasit.

BRUNEI
Capital: Bandar Seri Begawan
Area: 5,765 sq km (2,225 sq miles)
Population: 328,000
Languages: Malay, English
Religions: Muslim, Buddhist

CAMBODIA
Capital: Phnom Pénh
Area: 181,035 sq km
(69,881 sq miles)
Population: 11,200,000
Languages: Khmer
Religion: Buddhist

INDONESIA
Capital: Jakarta
Area: 1,904,569 sq km
(735,412 sq miles)
Population: 212,000,000
Language: Indonesian
Religion: Muslim

LAOS
Capital: Vientiane
Area: 236,800 sq km (91,435 sq miles)

Population: 5,400,000
Language: Lao
Religion: Buddhist

MALAYSIA
Capital: Kuala Lumpur
Area: 329,749 sq km
(127,326 sq miles)
Population: 22,200,000
Languages: Malay, English, Chinese
Religions: Muslim, Buddhist

PAPUA NEW GUINEA
Capital: Port Moresby
Area: 462,840 sq km
(178,716 sq miles)
Population: 4,800,000
Languages: English, numerous
others
Religion: Christian

PHILIPPINES
Capital: Manila
Area: 300,000 sq km
(115,839 sq miles)
Population: 76,000,000

Languages: Filipino, English,
Spanish
Religion: Christian

SINGAPORE
Capital: Singapore
Area: 618 sq km (239 sq miles)
Population: 3,600,000
Languages: Malay, Chinese, English
Religion: Taoist, Buddhist

THAILAND
Capital: Bangkok
Area: 513,115 sq km
(198,129 sq miles)
Population: 61,400,000
Language: Thai
Religion: Buddhist

VIETNAM
Capital: Ha Nôi
Area: 329,558 sq km
(127,252 sq miles)
Population: 79,800,000
Languages: Vietnamese, Chinese
Religion: Buddhist

B

C

MAP QUIZ

✦ Perahu fishing boats sail along the coast of which country?

✦ Offshore oil is responsible for the fabulous wealth of which tiny Southeast Asian nation?

✦ The Mekong River runs through two countries on the map. Can you name them?

✦ What sea lies off Vietnam?

✦ Where is the Buddhist temple of Angkor Wat?

D

E

F

TAIWAN

Rice terraces

MANILA

LUZON

PHILIPPINES

PHILIPPINES

Sugar cane

Cebu

Monkey-eating eagle

Coral reefs

MINDANAO

Davao

Zamboanga

Vinta boat

Coral reefs

CELEBES SEA

Coconuts

PACIFIC OCEAN

G

H

I

Toraja house

Shrimps

Sago palms

MOLUCCAS

Oil

Oil

Nutmeg

Sago palms

Tuna

Jayapura

Spirit house

Coconuts

CELEBES

Cloves

Coffee

Crabs

CERAM SEA

CERAM

Tree kangaroo

IRIAN JAYA

PUNCAK JAYA 5,040 m

NEW GUINEA

MT WILHELM 4,509 m

PAPUA NEW GUINEA

NEW BRITAIN

Ujungpandang

BANDA SEA

Irian Jaya native

Dancer and drum

ONESIA

Komodo dragon

Asmat warriors

Bird of paradise

PORT MORESBY

FLORES

Maize

DILI

PART OF EAST TIMOR

TIMOR

EAST TIMOR

ARAFURA SEA

PAPUA NEW GUINEA

UMBA

Kupang

TIMOR SEA

AUSTRALIA

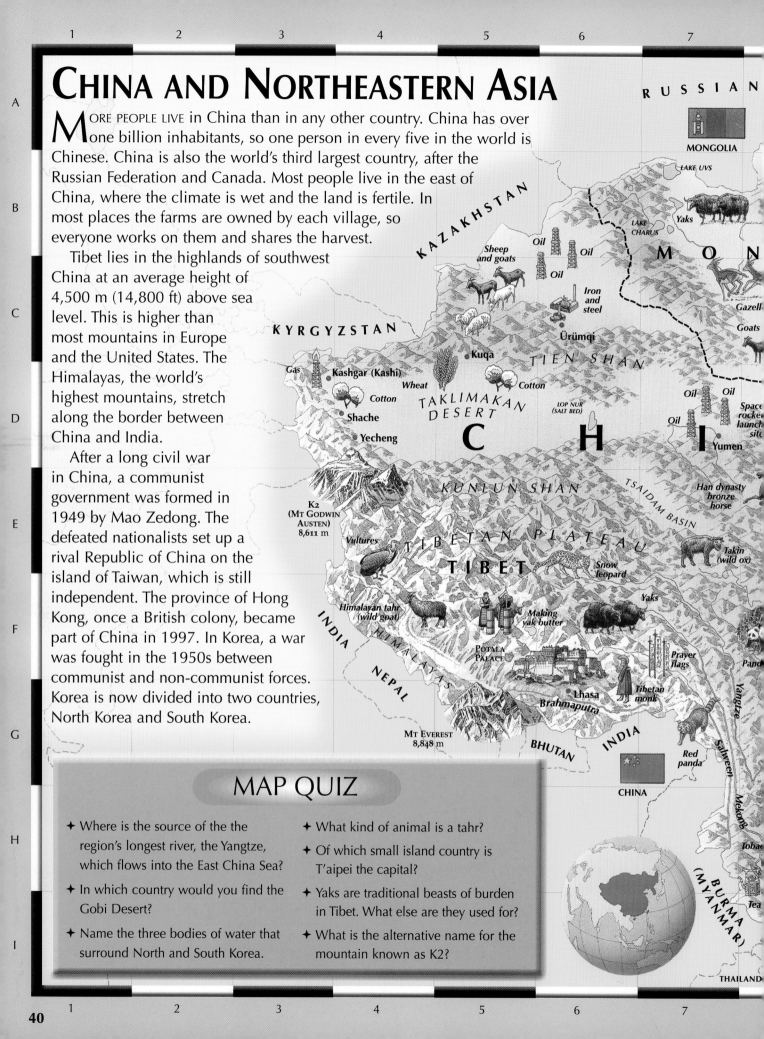

CHINA AND NORTHEASTERN ASIA

MORE PEOPLE LIVE in China than in any other country. China has over one billion inhabitants, so one person in every five in the world is Chinese. China is also the world's third largest country, after the Russian Federation and Canada. Most people live in the east of China, where the climate is wet and the land is fertile. In most places the farms are owned by each village, so everyone works on them and shares the harvest.

Tibet lies in the highlands of southwest China at an average height of 4,500 m (14,800 ft) above sea level. This is higher than most mountains in Europe and the United States. The Himalayas, the world's highest mountains, stretch along the border between China and India.

After a long civil war in China, a communist government was formed in 1949 by Mao Zedong. The defeated nationalists set up a rival Republic of China on the island of Taiwan, which is still independent. The province of Hong Kong, once a British colony, became part of China in 1997. In Korea, a war was fought in the 1950s between communist and non-communist forces. Korea is now divided into two countries, North Korea and South Korea.

MAP QUIZ

✦ Where is the source of the the region's longest river, the Yangtze, which flows into the East China Sea?

✦ In which country would you find the Gobi Desert?

✦ Name the three bodies of water that surround North and South Korea.

✦ What kind of animal is a tahr?

✦ Of which small island country is T'aipei the capital?

✦ Yaks are traditional beasts of burden in Tibet. What else are they used for?

✦ What is the alternative name for the mountain known as K2?

Map labels

RUSSIAN

MONGOLIA

LAKE UVS

KAZAKHSTAN

Yaks

LAKE CHARUS

M O N

Oil — Oil — Oil

Sheep and goats

Iron and steel

Gazell

KYRGYZSTAN

Goats

Ürümqi

TIEN SHAN

Gas

Kuqa

Kashgar (Kashi)

Wheat

Cotton

Oil — Oil

Cotton

TAKLIMAKAN DESERT

LOP NUR (SALT BED)

Shache

Oil

Yecheng

C H I

Yumen

Space rocket launch site

KUNLUN SHAN

TSAIDAM BASIN

Han dynasty bronze horse

K2 (MT GODWIN AUSTEN) 8,611 m

Vultures

TIBETAN PLATEAU

Takin (wild ox)

TIBET

Snow leopard

INDIA

Himalayan tahr (wild goat)

Yaks

Making yak butter

Prayer flags

Pand

HIMALAYAS

POTALA PALACE

NEPAL

Tibetan monk

Yangtze

Lhasa

Brahmaputra

MT EVEREST 8,848 m

INDIA

Red panda

Salween

BHUTAN

CHINA

Toba

BURMA (MYANMAR)

Mekong

Tea

THAILAND

FACTS AND FIGURES

The Great Wall of China, built to protect the northern border, is nearly 3,460 km (2,150 miles) long.

Longest river:
Yangtze (Chang Jiang), 6,300 km (3,915 miles).

Largest city:
Shanghai (China), 13,510,000.

The gateway to the Chaotain Palace in the historic city of Nanjing, formerly China's capital.

CHINA
Capital: Beijing (Peking)
Area: 9,598,055 sq km (3,704,863 sq miles)
Population: 1,300,000,000
Language: Chinese
Religions: Confucianist, Buddhist, Taoist, Muslim
Currency: Yuan
Government: Communist republic

MONGOLIA
Capital: Ulan Bator
Area: 1,565,000 sq km (604,247 sq miles)
Population: 2,700,000
Language: Mongolian
Religions: Buddhist, Lamaist, Muslim
Currency: Tugrik
Government: Republic

NORTH KOREA
Capital: P'yongyang
Area: 120,538 sq km (46,540 sq miles)
Population: 24,000,000
Language: Korean
Religions: Buddhist, Confucianist, Taoist
Currency: North Korean Won
Government: Communist republic

SOUTH KOREA
Capital: Seoul
Area: 99,016 sq km (38,230 sq miles)
Population: 46,800,000
Language: Korean
Religions: Buddhist, Confucianist, Christian
Currency: South Korean Won
Government: Multiparty Republic

TAIWAN
Capital: T'aipei
Area: 35,990 sq km (13,890 sq miles)
Population: 22,000,000
Language: Chinese
Religions: Buddhist, Taoist, Christian
Currency: Taiwan dollar
Government: Multiparty Republic

AFRICA

A FLAT PLATEAU broken by mountain ranges, Africa stretches about 4,000 km (2,500 miles) north and south of the equator. Dominating north Africa are the Mediterranean coastline and the Sahara Desert; to the south are the grasslands of east Africa, the rainforest of the Zaire basin and the farmlands of Kenya, Uganda and Tanzania.

Some African countries have agricultural economies: maize, coffee, tea, fruit, tobacco and cotton are typical crops. Others are rich in gold, diamonds, oil, copper and iron. Many regions, though, are desperately poor, and their people suffer constantly from disease and famine.

MAP QUIZ

+ The highest peak in Africa is Mt Kilimanjaro. Where is it?
+ In what country can you see the pyramids at Giza, which were built as tombs for ancient rulers?
+ Can you name the world's longest river, which flows through Africa into the Mediterranean Sea?
+ The largest desert on earth is also on this continent. What is it called?
+ What is a felucca?
+ Which country has three capital cities?

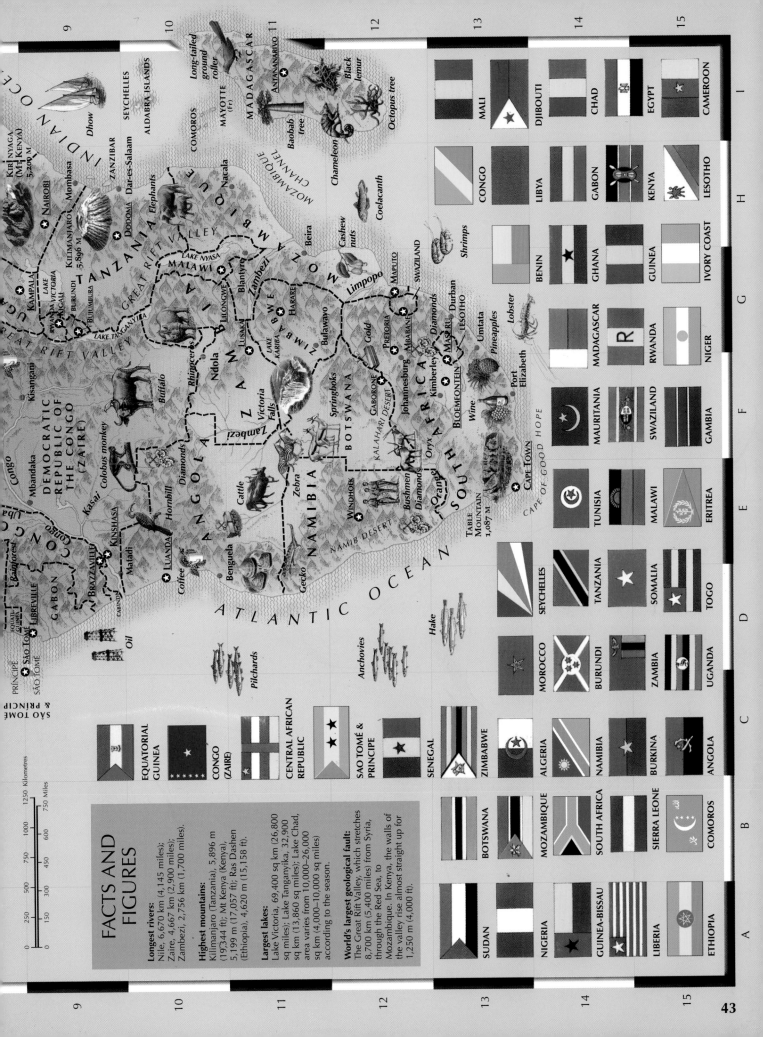

FACTS AND FIGURES

Longest rivers:
Nile, 6,670 km (4,145 miles); Zaire, 4,667 km (2,900 miles); Zambezi, 2,756 km (1,700 miles).

Highest mountains:
Kilimanjaro (Tanzania), 5,896 m (19,344 ft); Mt Kenya (Kenya), 5,199 m (17,057 ft); Ras Dashen (Ethiopia), 4,620 m (15,158 ft).

Largest lakes:
Lake Victoria, 69,400 sq km (26,800 sq miles); Lake Tanganyika, 32,900 sq km (13,860 sq miles); Lake Chad, area varies from 10,000–26,000 sq km (4,000–10,000 sq miles) according to the season.

World's largest geological fault:
The Great Rift Valley, which stretches 8,700 km (5,400 miles) from Syria, through the Red Sea, to Mozambique. In Kenya, the walls of the valley rise almost straight up for 1,250 m (4,000 ft).

Kilometres 0 250 500 750 1000 1250
Miles 0 150 300 450 600 750

Map labels

INDIAN OCEAN
ATLANTIC OCEAN
MOZAMBIQUE CHANNEL
CAPE OF GOOD HOPE

KIRI NYAGA (Mt KENYA) 5,200 M
Dhow
SEYCHELLES
ALDABRA ISLANDS
COMOROS
MAYOTTE (Fr)
MADAGASCAR
ANTANANARIVO
Long-tailed ground roller
Black lemur
Baobab tree
Octopus tree
Chameleon
Coelacanth
Cashew nuts
Shrimps
Lobster
Pineapples
Wine
Hake
Anchovies
Pilchards

NAIROBI
Mombasa
Zanzibar
Dar-es-Salaam
KAMPALA
UGANDA
Lake Victoria
RWANDA KIGALI
BURUNDI
BUJUMBURA
Lake Tanganyika
TANZANIA
DODOMA
Elephants
KILIMANJARO 5,896 M
GREAT RIFT VALLEY
LAKE NYASA
MALAWI
LILONGWE
Blantyre
Nacala
Beira
Zambezi
Limpopo
MAPUTO
SWAZILAND
MBABANE
Durban
Umtata
LESOTHO MASERU

DEMOCRATIC REPUBLIC OF THE CONGO (ZAIRE)
Kisangani
Mbandaka
Congo
Kasai
KINSHASA
Matadi
BRAZZAVILLE
CONGO
GABON
LIBREVILLE
EQUATORIAL GUINEA
SÃO TOMÉ & PRÍNCIPE
SÃO TOMÉ
Oil
Coffee
Gecko
Colobus monkey
Hornbill
Buffalo
Cattle
Rhinoceros
Diamonds
LUANDA
Benguela
Cabinda
ANGOLA
ZAMBIA
Lusaka
Ndola
LAKE KARIBA
ZIMBABWE
HARARE
Bulawayo
Gold
Springboks
Zebra
Victoria Falls
Zambezi
NAMIBIA
WINDHOEK
Bushmen
Diamonds
KALAHARI DESERT
BOTSWANA
GABORONE
Oryx
NAMIB DESERT
SOUTH AFRICA
PRETORIA
Johannesburg
Kimberley
BLOEMFONTEIN
Orange
CAPE TOWN
TABLE MOUNTAIN 1,087 M
Port Elizabeth

Flags

MALI — DJIBOUTI — CHAD — EGYPT — CAMEROON
CONGO — LIBYA — GABON — KENYA — LESOTHO
BENIN — GHANA — GUINEA — IVORY COAST
MADAGASCAR — RWANDA — NIGER
MAURITANIA — SWAZILAND — GAMBIA
TUNISIA — MALAWI — ERITREA
SEYCHELLES — TANZANIA — SOMALIA — TOGO
MOROCCO — BURUNDI — ZAMBIA — UGANDA
ZIMBABWE — ALGERIA — NAMIBIA — BURKINA — ANGOLA
SENEGAL
SAO TOMÉ & PRINCIPE
CENTRAL AFRICAN REPUBLIC
CONGO (ZAIRE)
EQUATORIAL GUINEA
BOTSWANA — MOZAMBIQUE — SOUTH AFRICA — SIERRA LEONE — COMOROS
SUDAN — NIGERIA — GUINEA-BISSAU — LIBERIA — ETHIOPIA

AUSTRALIA

AUSTRALIA IS A country and a continent. Much of it is hot and dry, especially in the sparsely populated central deserts. Most people live where the climate is wetter, east of the Great Dividing Range and on the island of Tasmania. Two-thirds of all Australians live in cities, particularly Sydney, Melbourne, and Brisbane. The population of Australia is only 17.9 million people, compared with 278 million in the United States.

Millions of years ago, Australia drifted away from the other continents, so many plants and animals that evolved there are not found anywhere else. Some mammals, such as kangaroos, are marsupials: they rear their young in pouches on their stomachs.

The first inhabitants appeared about 100,000 years ago and Aboriginal Australians are their descendants. Europeans did not arrive until 200 years ago. Since 1945 the population has doubled, with people coming to Australia from many parts of the world.

MAP QUIZ

+ Uluru (Ayers Rock) is near which group of mountains?

+ Name the two coastal cities joined by the Indian-Pacific Railway.

+ Where would you find an international opera house whose design was inspired by sailing ships?

+ The Port Arthur Penal Settlement is located on which island?

+ What is the common name for an Australian wild dog?

+ Which remote town provides a base for the flying doctor service?

+ Can you find the place where a meteorite landed in Australia?

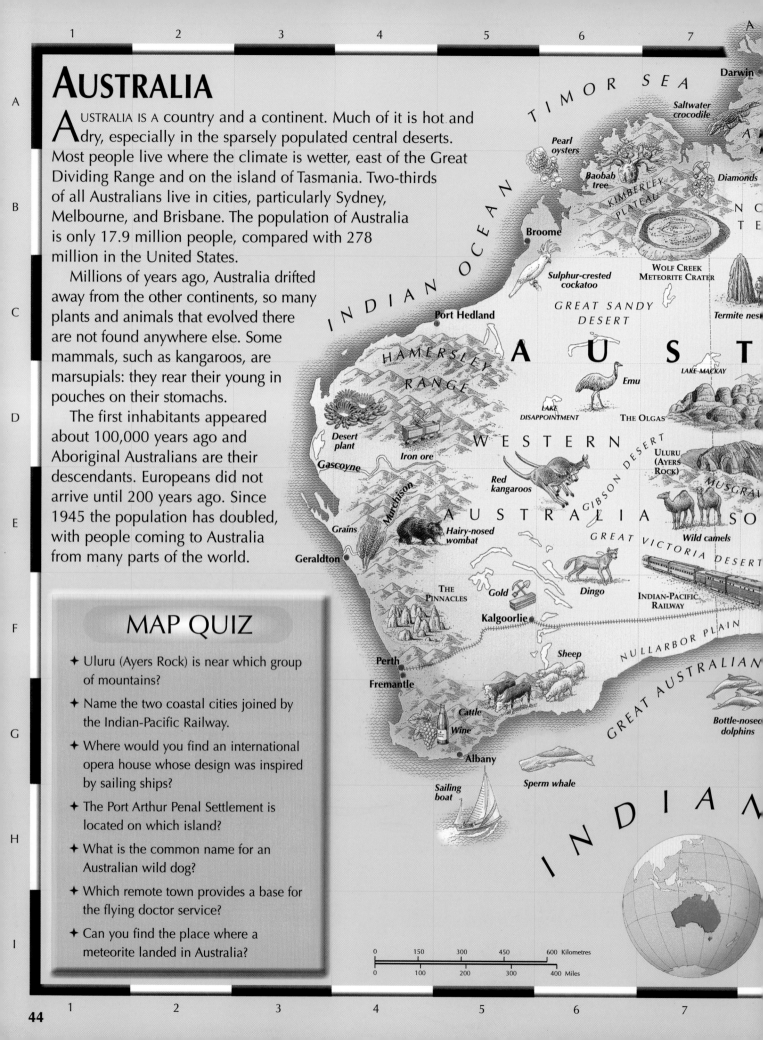

Map labels:
TIMOR SEA
Darwin
Saltwater crocodile
Pearl oysters
Baobab tree
Diamonds
KIMBERLEY PLATEAU
Broome
INDIAN OCEAN
Sulphur-crested cockatoo
WOLF CREEK METEORITE CRATER
GREAT SANDY DESERT
Termite nest
Port Hedland
AUST
HAMERSLEY RANGE
Emu
LAKE MACKAY
LAKE DISAPPOINTMENT
THE OLGAS
Desert plant
WESTERN
GIBSON DESERT
ULURU (AYERS ROCK)
Iron ore
MUSGRA
Gascoyne
Red kangaroos
Murchison
AUSTRALIA
SO
Grains
Hairy-nosed wombat
GREAT VICTORIA DESERT
Wild camels
Geraldton
THE PINNACLES
Gold
Dingo
INDIAN-PACIFIC RAILWAY
Kalgoorlie
NULLARBOR PLAIN
Perth
Sheep
Fremantle
GREAT AUSTRALIAN
Cattle
Bottle-nosed dolphins
Wine
Albany
Sperm whale
Sailing boat
INDIAN

Scale:
0 150 300 450 600 Kilometres
0 100 200 300 400 Miles

RA SEA

TORRES STRAIT

Aboriginal dancers

GROOTE EYLANDT

GULF OF CARPENTARIA

Coral reef

Aboriginal cave paintings

Green turtle

CORAL SEA

Water buffalo

MACDONNELL RANGES

BARKLY TABLELAND

THE DEVIL'S MARBLES

Cattle

Sugar cane

Cairns

GREAT BARRIER REEF

Coral reef

Scuba diving

Road train

Townsville

GREAT DIVIDING RANGE

Mount Isa

Cattle

Coal

Mackay

Coral reef

RALIA

Sheep

Sugar cane

Alice Springs

QUEENSLAND

Flying doctor

SIMPSON DESERT

Sheep

Rockhampton

Coal

Wallabies

GREAT DIVIDING RANGE

RANGES

TH AUSTRALIA

Grains

Brisbane skyscrapers

Opals

LAKE EYRE

Sheep

Lyrebird

Brisbane

Surfers Paradise

LAKE TORRENS

NEW

Sapphires

Pineapples

Woomera

River red gum tree

Darling

Koalas

Bananas

FLINDERS RANGES

SOUTH

Tamworth

LAKE GAIRDNER

Broken Hill

Windsurfing

Port Augusta

Kookaburra

WALES

Iron and steel

Whyalla

Paddle steamer

Coal

Newcastle

Iron and steel

Platypus

Sydney

Cars

Mildura

Murrumbidgee

Wollongong

Adelaide

Murray

Wagga Wagga

CANBERRA

SYDNEY OPERA HOUSE AND BRIDGE

Shipbuilding

Pelicans

VICTORIA

Albury

Wine

Bendigo

Skiing

Surfing

Great white shark

Ballarat

AUSTRALIAN CAPITAL TERRITORY

Timber

Melbourne

Geelong

Rock lobster

Fairy penguins

Horse racing

Sharks

BASS STRAIT

Sailing

OCEAN

TASMANIA

Tasmanian devil

TASMAN SEA

AUSTRALIA

Apples

Hobart

PORT ARTHUR PENAL SETTLEMENT

FACTS AND FIGURES

View of Sydney harbour, with its famous bridge and opera house.

Largest cities:
Sydney, 3,698,500; Melbourne, 3,153,500; Brisbane, 1,327,000.

Longest river:
Murray-Darling, 3,750 km (2,330 miles).

Largest lake:
Lake Eyre (dry for part of the year), max. of 9,583 sq km (3,700 sq miles).

World's leading wool producer:
Australia produces 25 per cent of the world's wool. There are around 10 sheep per person in Australia.

World's longest fence:
Made of wire mesh, the dingo-proof fence around the main sheep grazing areas in Queensland is more than 2,500 km (1,553 miles) long.

Koalas, a protected species, are found only in Australia.

AUSTRALIA
Capital: Canberra
Area: 7,686,848 sq km (2,967,207 sq miles)
Population: 17,900,000
Language: English
Religion: Christian
Currency: Australian dollar

STATES AND TERRITORIES:
NEW SOUTH WALES
State capital: Sydney
Area: 801,430 sq km (309,350 sq miles)
Population: 6,039,000

NORTHERN TERRITORY
State capital: Darwin
Area: 1,346,200 sq km (519,635 sq miles)
Population: 195,100

QUEENSLAND
State capital: Brisbane
Area: 1,727,000 sq km (666,620 sq miles)
Population: 3,369,000

SOUTH AUSTRALIA
State capital: Adelaide
Area: 984,380 sq km (379,981 sq miles)
Population: 1,428,000

TASMANIA
State capital: Hobart
Area: 68,330 sq km (26,375 sq miles)
Population: 460,000

VICTORIA
State capital: Melbourne
Area: 227,600 sq km (87,855 sq miles)
Population: 4,373,500

WESTERN AUSTRALIA
State capital: Perth
Area: 2,525,500 sq km (974,845 sq miles)
Population: 1,726,000

AUSTRALIAN CAPITAL TERRITORY
State capital: Canberra
Area: 2,432 sq km (939 sq miles)
Population: 299,000

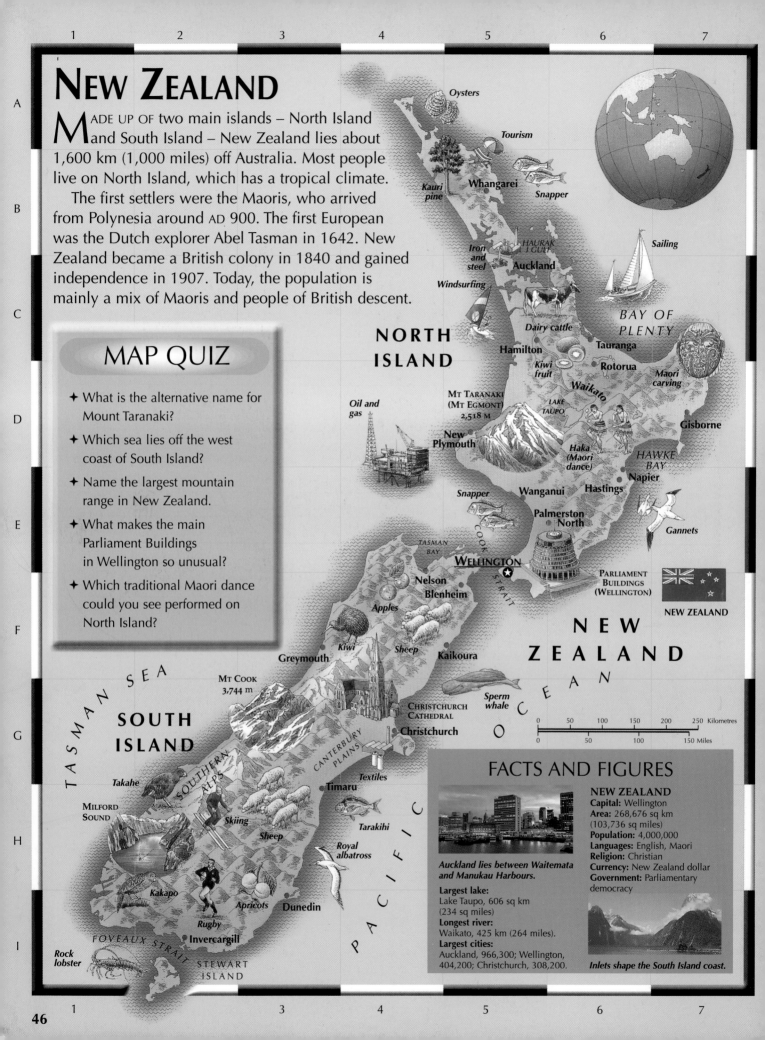

NEW ZEALAND

MADE UP OF two main islands – North Island and South Island – New Zealand lies about 1,600 km (1,000 miles) off Australia. Most people live on North Island, which has a tropical climate.

The first settlers were the Maoris, who arrived from Polynesia around AD 900. The first European was the Dutch explorer Abel Tasman in 1642. New Zealand became a British colony in 1840 and gained independence in 1907. Today, the population is mainly a mix of Maoris and people of British descent.

MAP QUIZ

✦ What is the alternative name for Mount Taranaki?

✦ Which sea lies off the west coast of South Island?

✦ Name the largest mountain range in New Zealand.

✦ What makes the main Parliament Buildings in Wellington so unusual?

✦ Which traditional Maori dance could you see performed on North Island?

NORTH ISLAND

Oysters
Tourism
Kauri pine
Whangarei
Snapper
HAURAKI GULF
Iron and steel
Auckland
Sailing
Windsurfing
BAY OF PLENTY
Dairy cattle
Hamilton
Tauranga
Kiwi fruit
Rotorua
Waikato
Maori carving
Oil and gas
MT TARANAKI (MT EGMONT) 2,518 M
LAKE TAUPO
New Plymouth
Haka (Maori dance)
Gisborne
HAWKE BAY
Snapper
Wanganui
Hastings
Napier
Palmerston North
Gannets
TASMAN BAY
COOK STRAIT
WELLINGTON
Nelson
Blenheim
PARLIAMENT BUILDINGS (WELLINGTON)
Apples
NEW ZEALAND
Kiwi
Sheep
Kaikoura
Greymouth
NEW ZEALAND
MT COOK 3,744 m
Sperm whale
OCEAN
CHRISTCHURCH CATHEDRAL
Christchurch
TASMAN SEA
SOUTHERN ALPS
CANTERBURY PLAINS
SOUTH ISLAND
Takahe
Textiles
Timaru
MILFORD SOUND
Tarakihi
Skiing
Sheep
Royal albatross
Kakapo
Apricots
Dunedin
Rugby
PACIFIC
Invercargill
FOVEAUX STRAIT
Rock lobster
STEWART ISLAND

FACTS AND FIGURES

Auckland lies between Waitemata and Manukau Harbours.

Largest lake:
Lake Taupo, 606 sq km (234 sq miles)
Longest river:
Waikato, 425 km (264 miles).
Largest cities:
Auckland, 966,300; Wellington, 404,200; Christchurch, 308,200.

NEW ZEALAND
Capital: Wellington
Area: 268,676 sq km (103,736 sq miles)
Population: 4,000,000
Languages: English, Maori
Religion: Christian
Currency: New Zealand dollar
Government: Parliamentary democracy

Inlets shape the South Island coast.

0 50 100 150 200 250 Kilometres
0 50 100 150 Miles

INDEX

This index contains the most important place and feature names. The page number is given in **bold** type after the place name. The grid reference follows in lighter type.